Expressing Creativity in Preschool

From the editors of *Teaching Young Children*

Expressing Creativity
in Preschool

From the editors of *Teaching Young Children*

National Association for the Education of Young Children
Washington, DC

National Association for the Education
of Young Children

Through its publications program, the National Association for the Education of Young Children (NAEYC) provides a forum for discussion of major issues and ideas in the early childhood field, with the hope of provoking thought and promoting professional growth. The views expressed or implied in this book are not necessarily those of the Association or its members.

NAEYC Publishing

Chief Publishing Officer
Derry Koralek

Editor-in-Chief
Kathy Charner

Director of Creative Services
Edwin C. Malstrom

Managing Editor
Mary Jaffe

Senior Editor
Holly Bohart

Senior Graphic Designer
Malini Dominey

Designer
Victoria Moy

Associate Editor
Meghan Dombrink-Green

Associate Editor
Elizabeth Wegner

Assistant Editor
Lauren Baker

Editorial Assistant
Ryan Smith

Credits

Cover design: Edwin C. Malstrom

Photographs: Copyright © Sandra Floyd: v (middle right), 28; Jacky Howell: 109; Beth Ann Moore: 62; NAEYC: vi (middle left), 55 (bottom), 77; Elizabeth Nichols: 4, 13, 93; Marilyn Nolt: 95 (top); Mary O'Connor: 54; Karen Phillips: v (middle left), vi (middle right), 17, 18, 19, 32, 34 (top right), 55 (top), 66, 67, 69, 76, 104, 113, 114, 115; Michael J. Rosen: 66; Shari Schmidt: vii (middle) 7, 94, 95 (bottom right); Ellen Senisi: cover (center and right), 37, 106, 107; Kathy Sible: 95 (bottom left); University of Maine Center for Community Inclusion and Disability Studies: 19; Susan Woog Wagner (© NAEYC): cover (left) 41, 43, 62; Kevin Wauligman: vi (top), 40–45, 63; Maria Wynne: v (top), 6, 7, 8

Courtesy of article authors: v (bottom), vi (bottom), vii (top and bottom), 20–25, 31, 33, 34 (left), 34 (bottom right), 35, 56–58, 70–71, 74–76, 101–3, 114

Illustrations: Copyright © Jennifer O'Connell

Expressing Creativity in Preschool.

Library of Congress Control Number: 2014945038
ISBN: 978-1-938113-08-6
Item 7225

CONTENTS

1 INTRODUCTION
by Meghan Dombrink-Green

ART

4   The Value of Open-Ended Art
by Christine Maynard and Kara J. Ketter

10   Art Learning Center
by Laura J. Colker

14   A Place for Weaving
by Laura J. Colker

18   Painting Without Brushes
by Meghan Dombrink-Green

20   Using Collage to Encourage Creativity, High-Level Thinking, and Conversation!
by Triada Samaras and Janis Strasser, With Michele J. Russo

26   Books With Engaging Illustrations
by Susan Friedman

28   Collecting, Painting, and Studying Leaves
by Jolyn Blank and Ellie Wastin

31   Splatter Paint
by Violet McGillen

34   Discovering Science While Exploring Art
by Sara Starbuck and Leigh Tyler Marshall-Oliver

38   Art Learning Center Checklist
by Laura J. Colker

MUSIC AND MOVEMENT

40 **The Power of Creative Dance**
by Connie Bergstein Dow

46 **Music and Movement Learning Center**
by Laura J. Colker

50 **A Place for Making Musical Instruments**
by Laura J. Colker

54 **Promoting Music Play**
by Kristen M. Kemple, Jacqueline J. Batey, and Lynn C. Hartle

56 **A Stage for the Playground: An Outdoor Music Center**
by Carol Garboden Murray

59 **Learning in Motion**
by Donna Furmanek

60 **Books That Feature Song Lyrics**
by Lauren Baker

62 **Dance Stories**
by Connie Bergstein Dow

65 **Attend a Live Performance**
by Susan Friedman

68 **Learn, Sing, Play: Nature-Related, Low-Cost Music Activities**
by Petra Kern and Beth McLaughlin

72 **Music and Movement Learning Center Checklist**
by Laura J. Colker

DRAMATIC PLAY

74 Oral Storytelling: Building Community Through Dialogue, Engagement, and Problem Solving
by Doriet Berkowitz

80 Dramatic Play Learning Center
by Amy Laura Dombro

84 A Place for Puppets
by Laura J. Colker

88 Ways to Make Puppets
by Meghan Dombrink-Green

92 Pretend Play Leads to Real-Life Learning
by Laura J. Colker

96 Books That Tell Folktales
by Lauren Baker

98 Creating and Using Prop Boxes
by Derry Koralek

101 Engineering With *The Three Little Pigs*
by Maureen Ingram

104 Using Improvisational Play to Support Social Skills
by Barbara E. O'Neill

109 What's in Your Dramatic Play Center?
compiled by Lauren Baker

110 Dramatic Play Learning Center Checklist
by Laura J. Colker

111 CREDITS

113 ABOUT THE AUTHORS

Introduction

Meghan Dombrink-Green

It started years ago when I was in college. I would write my parents letters and decorate the envelope with designs, doodles, and stick figures. Sometimes the stick figure would wave, other times the stick figure would use thought bubbles to share some of the things I was thinking that day. On occasion the stick figure scenes carried from one side of the envelope to the other. In the last few years, however, my decorated envelopes to my parents have dwindled. But each time my mother calls she reminds me how much she enjoys—and would enjoy—one of those envelopes.

Pablo Picasso said "Every child is an artist. The problem is staying an artist when you grow up." Today that's true for me, but I want to change that. So the next time I write my parents a letter, I will decorate the envelope first. Maybe I'll even draw my letter instead of writing it. I'll add new materials and try some colored markers.

And this will be my small attempt to find my creative self and share it with the people I love.

When is the last time you did something creative? If you're thinking back more than a month ago, pause for a moment. When was the last time you painted with the children in your program, embellished a friend's birthday card with a doodle, or added a new ingredient to a favorite recipe? Chances are you've been more creative than you realize. Now consider the how, why, and when of being creative. Creativity needs materials, time, and encouragement—and that is what teachers can provide for children.

As an educator, you can help build, strengthen, and grow children's learning and creativity. When children have opportunities to be creative, their language, social, and cognitive skills grow (Bodrova & Leong 2012). Additionally, creativity is an essential skill for children and adults in the twenty-first century (Partnership for 21st Century Skills 2009).

About This Book

From materials to activities, dance moves to field trips, the content in this book offers practical strategies and engaging visuals to help teachers support preschoolers' creativity. Ideas are organized into three sections: art, music and movement, and dramatic play. Each section features ideas and activities related to that topic, as well as useful tips so teachers can immediately try these strategies in the classroom. At the end of each section is a checklist to help you review how you and the children use the different learning centers.

Through bright drawings, the learning center pieces showcase innovative ways to design, arrange, and implement best practices. The accompanying text identifies what children do and learn in a particular center, how the center can include children's families and cultures, tips for setting up the center, and suggestions for stretching your budget.

The tips for supporting dual language learners describe ways to help children who are learning two or more languages at the same time. These tips were written by Karen N. Nemeth, author of *Basics of Supporting Dual Language Learners* (NAEYC, 2012).

The Reflective Questions help you think about yourself as a teacher and about the specific children in your program. The Reflective Questions Thinking Lens®, which is a way of examining your teaching practice, comes from Deb Curtis and colleagues at Harvest Resources Associates, LLC.

The ideas in this book support the development and learning of all preschoolers. For example, while some children may prefer to play alone or spend all their time in one center, almost all children have a favorite story that can be expanded through pretending and dramatic play (Wanerman 2010). Teachers can use these suggestions to individualize activities and scaffold children's learning.

As you read through this book, note your favorite ideas by adding stickies or folding down page corners. Or try a ribbon. Perhaps a scrap paper with space for notes. By the time you finish, you'll have a lot of marked pages and new ways to build on the excellence you bring to the classroom.

So when you think about children's creativity and your own creativity, remember these words from Pablo Picasso: "Every child is an artist." And when teachers offer children the right activities and supports to express their creativity, they help children continue to be artists as adults.

REFERENCES

Leong, D.J., & E. Bodrova. 2012. "Assessing and Scaffolding: Make-Believe Play." *Young Children* 67 (1): 28–34.

Partnership for 21st Century Skills. 2009. "P21 Framework Definitions." www.p21.org/storage/documents/P21_Framework_Definitions.pdf.

Wanerman, T. 2010. "Using Story Drama With Young Preschoolers." *Young Children* 65 (2): 20–28.

Art

The Value of Open-Ended Art

Christine Maynard and Kara J. Ketter

Five-year-old Andrew works at the easel with a few cups of paint, a big sheet of white paper, and his own imagination to guide him. Standing back from the easel to view his work, he looks deep in thought.

"What are you thinking, Andrew?" I ask.

"Well, I was thinking that with all these paintings, maybe we could have a gallery."

"A what?"

"A gallery."

"Oh, you mean like an art show?"

"YES! We can have an art show and our moms and dads can come! We can make signs to tell them!" Andrew's imagination and love of art have been unleashed.

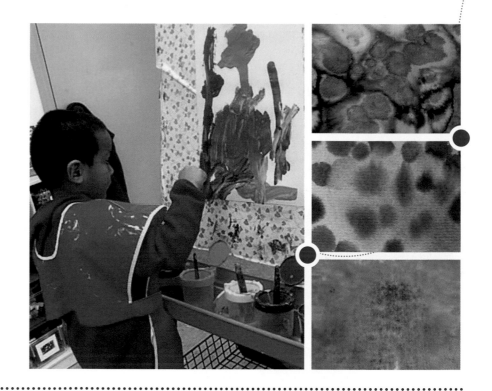

When I (Christine) was first learning to be a teacher, I drew shapes for children to color in. During my year teaching Andrew, however, I encountered a number of influences that challenged this thinking. My supervisor, the preschool program coordinator, encouraged me to provide fewer crafts and more open-ended materials to see how the children would experiment. For me, this was a process of giving the children more and more control. Ultimately, having the power to decide what to do, how to do it, and what to do with the end product greatly fueled Andrew's learning.

Why Open-Ended?

Young children actively construct their knowledge by interacting with the world around them (Piaget 1928). This means that they need to touch, see, explore, and manipulate objects and ideas to develop and learn. Young children should have "daily opportunities for creative expression" (Copple & Bredekamp 2009). Open-ended art is the perfect outlet for young children to process the information they take in.

Creative, open-ended art taps into three key developmental areas for young children. **First**, it allows an emotional outlet, encouraging children's active expression and communication (Pitri 2001). **Second**, it builds executive function (the ability to plan, monitor, and adjust behaviors to achieve a goal). This skill is important for focusing attention, problem solving, managing one's own behavior, and overall learning in school and in life (National Institutes of Health 2012). Open-ended art materials challenge children to plan and solve problems as they create. They can focus their attention on an engaging task of their choosing and follow through to a conclusion. This may be an end product or simply the end of an experience (Pitri 2001). Children use these same planning, problem solving, attending, and persevering skills to write, do math problems, and solve disagreements with classmates. **Third**, open-ended art helps to build, strengthen, and refine motor skills necessary for buttoning, zipping, writing, and typing.

Materials to Encourage Open-Ended Art

Keep available all the time	Add or remove to follow children's interests	Include based on special events or interests (a class trip to the beach, a school visit from a florist)
• Pencils • Crayons • Markers • Glue • Scissors • Playdough or clay • Paint • Brushes • Envelopes • Various types of paper, such as construction, wallpaper scraps, tissue, newsprint	• Cardboard boxes, tubes, shapes • Ribbon, yarn, string • Wrapping paper • Wire • Beads • Wood pieces • Pom-poms • Crepe paper • Buttons • Pipe cleaners • Stamps and ink • Painting tools, such as toothbrushes, toothpicks, tongue depressors, cotton balls, cotton swabs, feathers	• Leaves, sticks, pinecones, acorns • Biodegradable packing peanuts • Flowers and flower petals • Fabric scraps • Sand • Shells • Rocks • Toy cars, toy animals, bubble wrap, and other items for texture painting • Recycled items such as plastic bottles, bottle caps, newspapers

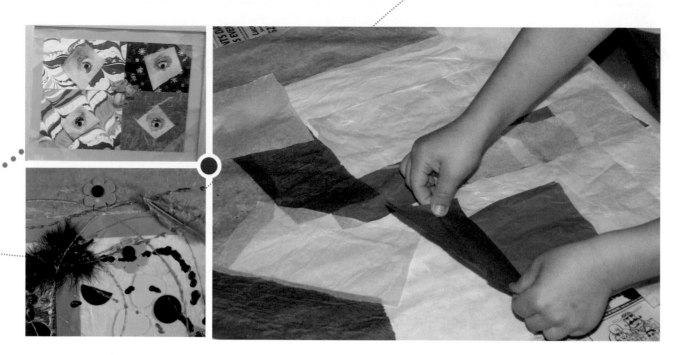

How do open-ended art experiences offer so many opportunities for learning? Consider the difference between open-ended and close-ended questions. Close-ended questions, such as "What animal is this?" or "Did you have fun?," tend to result in one-word answers and limit children's thinking. However, open-ended questions and prompts—such as "How do you think this animal builds a home?" or "Tell me about what you are building"— challenge children to use creative and critical thinking skills. This same concept applies to close-ended and open-ended art. Close-ended projects such as coloring in a coloring book or gluing precut pieces to make a craft may support fine motor skills, but open-ended art builds these skills *while* challenging children's creativity and critical thinking.

Seeing this contrast convinced me about open-ended art. I had been trained to provide theme-based crafts with everyone doing the same project. As a result, I often grew stressed trying to convince all of the children to do the art. They in turn were upset because they were not interested in the predefined stars that had taken me hours to cut out.

Finally I stopped trying to force art and started offering open-ended materials. By observing children at work, I gained information and used it to make decisions about what materials to provide. Children created more art than I had thought possible. They painted sheet after sheet when art interested them and chose other activities when they were not as interested. I also saw more children choosing to create art. Overall the children were happier, I was less stressed, and the art processes and products were richer, as children explored color, texture, and tools.

Planning Open-Ended Art Experiences

Teachers can provide a variety of inviting materials that children can use in their creations. In addition, teachers can plan specific activities that are open-ended by nature. As you consider an activity, ask the following questions to determine if it is truly open-ended.

1. What is my goal?

Goals should focus on the activity's process rather than the product (Kohl 1994). Consider the different ways a child might use the materials. Perhaps the goal is for the children to mix various colors of paint to make new hues. Another goal could be for the children to enhance their fine motor skills while experimenting with drawing tools of various thicknesses. Maybe the goal is for the children to communicate in a new way by telling a story or expressing a feeling through art.

2. Will the children be able to make significant choices on their own? Are the children taking the lead in this activity or is the teacher?

Giving children choices opens up their creativity without setting limits. To determine if the activity allows children to take the lead, ask yourself, "How many decisions have I made for them?" Have you told them what to paint, what colors to use, what surfaces to paint on? Have you decided what each end product should resemble by giving them a model to copy? If so, let go of these limits so the children can make choices on their own. A child's goal may be to explore textures while painting with different tools, rather than painting something specific. Remember, in open-ended art the process matters most.

3. Are there enough materials to encourage creative exploration?

There is no right number of materials for any given art experience. In fact, how much variety you include may depend on the amount of experience the children have with the medium or tools they are exploring. For example, if this is their first time using wire for sculpture, begin with a few different lengths of wire so children have time and freedom to get comfortable with manipulating the material. If they have plenty of experience with wire, offer small wire-working tools and items like beads or metal nuts and washers so children can explore their interests and creativity.

4. Is there enough time for thorough exploration?

The creative process takes time as children explore new and different ways to use the materials. They need plenty of time to work. Keep the schedule flexible so children can come and go as they please. Children can decide for themselves when their work is complete.

Conclusion

We incorporated Andrew's idea for an art show into our end-of-year celebration. This gave the children an opportunity to display their drawings, paintings, and collages. We overheard a few children ask their parents, "Do you like it?," while many more told their parents the stories behind their art.

You can find joy and delight by observing, taking photos, studying work samples, and reflecting as children engage in art experiences. Ask yourself questions like these using a Thinking Lens.

Know Yourself

Can you think of a time when you made a change in your teaching practices? What did you do and what did you learn? Are there other changes you would like to make? What can you learn about change from the author's description of her transformation?

Are you drawn to crafts and their orderliness? Do you find it pleasing to offer families and others a recognizable item as proof of learning? How might you combine your goals with providing children with open-ended art experiences?

Find the Details of Children's Competence

Demonstrate to yourself and families the value of open-ended art experiences by observing children engaged in them. Look for examples of children's strengths and competencies. What do you think is valuable about this experience? How can you share the story of children's competencies with families?

Seek the Children's Point of View

Observe children engaged with open-ended art materials. What are children drawn to and delighted by? How do their actions demonstrate their thinking and understandings? What skills and competencies do you see that reflect your planned goals?

Examine the Environment

Assess the kinds of materials and experiences you have available for children. Which ones allow children to explore and discover through their own initiative, using their own ideas and understandings? What might you change or add?

REFERENCES

Copple, C., & S. Bredekamp, eds. 2009. *Developmentally Appropriate Practice in Early Childhood Programs Serving Children From Birth Through Age 8*. 3rd ed. Washington, DC: NAEYC.

Kohl, M. 1994. *Preschool Art: It's the Process, Not the Product*. Beltsville, MD: Gryphon House.

National Institutes of Health. 2012. *NIH Toolbox Training Manual*. www.nihtoolbox.org/HowDoI/HowToAdministerTheToolbox/Pages/TrainingManual.aspx.

Piaget, J. 1928. *The Child's Conception of the World*. New York: Routledge.

Pitri, E. 2001. "The Role of Artistic Play in Problem Solving." *Art Education* 54 (3): 46–51.

Art Learning Center

Laura J. Colker

What Children Do and Learn

Language and Literacy
- Learn vocabulary: *color (bright, intense, dull, muted); line (wavy, curved); texture (rough, raised)* in English and their home languages.
- Write signs: *Please save Tamara's mobile.*
- Create and use recipe cards for making playdough and other art materials.
- Look at books about art techniques and artists.
- Describe and discuss children's own artwork and the art of other artists.

Math
- Experiment with balance as they make mobiles and stabiles (abstract sculptures).
- Make patterns with materials.

Science
- Explore the properties and effects of light.
- Experiment with mixing paint colors to make new shades.

Social Studies
- Learn from a classroom demonstration of an art technique, discussion, and hands-on experience led by a parent or local artist.
- Recycle art materials—draw on both sides of the paper, save paper scraps, and use found materials in collages.

Physical
- Develop eye-hand coordination.
- Practice the tripod grasp, later used for writing.
- Use tools such as scissors, brushes, and hole punchers.

Setup Tips

- Locate near a sink in a spot with lots of natural light.
- Check all labels. Some art materials are not safe for use by young children.
- Display reproductions of culturally diverse art. Include a wide range of styles, techniques, and media.
- Set up an easel outdoors and bring a basket of art materials. Incorporate sunlight and shadows in art projects.

Budget Stretchers

- Gather leaves, pods, pinecones, feathers, and flowers. Set up a recycling bin to collect items such as paper scraps, ribbons, buttons, magazines, and old photos.
- Ask home improvement stores for donations of brushes, glue, scissors, and the like. Out-of-date wallpaper sample books are great for making collages, cards, book covers, and more.

- Frame and display children's art, with their assistance. Framing can be as simple as mounting the work on a larger piece of construction paper. Children can help build frames using matting, Styrofoam, or wood. Some programs invest in inexpensive plastic frames to use over and over.
- Take actual or virtual field trips to art museums. Ask the education staff/docents to help you plan the visit so children can see art that features the cultures, techniques, and styles they've been exploring.
- Include art appreciation. Ask questions that encourage children to focus on techniques, images, colors, and messages—in their own art and that of others. How did you decide what colors to use in your painting? What do you see in this quilt? How do you feel when you look at this painting?

Include Children's Families and Cultures

- Invite families to share artwork that is representative of their home cultures.
- Ask families to suggest art ideas and materials. Invite parent volunteers to talk with children about their artwork—both the process of creating art and the products: paintings, weavings, collages, and so on.

A Place for Weaving

Laura J. Colker

A place for weaving, housed in the art center, offers children opportunities to create with a wide variety of materials. Children can explore textures and weaving techniques while working on individual or group projects.

Materials—Weaving requires a loom or other frame, items to thread in and out, and things to decorate or enhance the weavings.

Weaving

- Weave on real looms or make them using the items shown here or chipboard, mat board, potholder frames, plastic baskets, driftwood, tree branches, coat hangers, mesh kitchen bags, garden mesh, fence posts, rakes, or old picture frames.
- Weave with string, rope, yarn, raffia, straws, pipe cleaners, old ties and scarves, strips of paper, fabric or foam, crepe paper streamers, ribbons, potholder loops, dried grasses, or anything else that works.
- Enhance weavings by attaching buttons, feathers, glitter, beads, pom-poms, and fresh or dried flowers, weeds, leaves, and nuts.

Math

- Become aware of position in space by stapling yarn strips to one another on a cardboard frame.
- Measure and cut pieces of yarn or paper the length or width of a loom.
- Create a pattern by weaving pipe cleaners through paper strips.

Fine Motor Development

- Use small muscles to place loops onto prongs of potholder frame.
- Strengthen eye and hand coordination by pulling ribbon through vertical strands.
- Use scissors to cut yarn for weaving.

Language and Literacy

- Use books to find information by reading about Navajo blankets and then weaving with similar colors.
- Learn new words such as *loom*, *warp*, and *weft*.
- Understand that words and pictures go to-gether while returning materials to labeled containers.

- Look for old ties, yarn, scarves, sashes, fabric, and belts at thrift shops and yard sales.
- Ask families to save wire hangers and mesh bags to be washed and used as weaving frames.
- Hold a family workshop for making inexpensive looms. Here are some ideas:

  —www.simplifiedbuilding.com/projects/pvc-pipe-loom
  —www.montessoriworld.org/handwork/weave/weaving3.html
  —www.africancrafts.com/davilojo/ed/lesson2.htm
  —http://unplugyourkids.com/2009/01/11/picture-frame-loom
  —http://progressiveearlychildhoodeducation.blogspot.com/2010/10/getting-our-weave-on.html

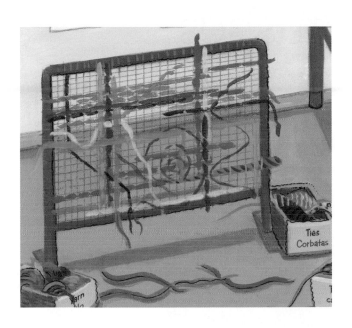

- Ask families to share weavings representative of their cultures to display in the art center.
- Invite family members to join in class weaving projects, perhaps incorporating special items such as an old piece of jewelry or a family photo.

Setup Tips

- Locate near a window, where natural light will allow children to see colors and designs.
- Place shelving under and on top of the table to conserve space.
- Set up a large frame or loom so children can spontaneously weave when inspiration hits them.
- Weave outdoors on a chain-link fence or set up plastic mesh fencing for a group weaving project. Provide weaving materials that can withstand rain and wind.

Painting Without Brushes

Meghan Dombrink-Green

Painting with brushes is fun, but there are lots of other ways to create. Try items that have different textures, shapes, and sizes. Children will enjoy using regular objects in new ways.

1 Boots
Ask children to bring in old boots or buy some at yard sales. Have them dip the boots in trays of paint or paint the soles using sponges. Then let the children stamp the boots on paper.

2 Feathers
Buy long feathers at a craft store. Their texture, weight, and length make for a unique painting experience.

3 Lids
Use recycled lids from plastic containers as circle stamps. Children can make excellent prints in different sizes and colors.

4 Marbles
Place a piece of paper in a large box top, add a dollop of paint, and drop in some marbles. Children will enjoy tilting the box and watching the marbles make fun designs as they roll around.

5 **Nylon stockings**
Fill women's knee-high stockings with pebbles, acorns, or sand. Have children dip the stockings in paint and bounce them on a table covered with paper.

6 **Rollers**
Invite children to pretend they are painters painting a house. Rollers spread colors in an easy motion.

7 **Squeeze bottles**
Use a bottle with a secure cap—otherwise there may be an explosion of color! As children apply different amounts of pressure, they will see how their strength affects how much paint comes out of the bottle.

8 **Straws**
Provide diluted paint or pre-mixed watercolors, and have children blow through straws to direct the paint. Straight straws work best.

9 **Body parts**
Paint with hands, feet, elbows, fingertips. Body parts are great for painting!

10 **Baking tins**
Make great patterns with cupcake tins. After children paint the bottom of each section, they can stamp the tin on paper.

Using Collage to Encourage Creativity, High-Level Thinking, and Conversation!

Triada Samaras and Janis Strasser, With Michele J. Russo

Collage is an ideal way to introduce preschool children to basic art concepts. You'll also give them an engaging open-ended art experience. To ensure success, choose materials wisely, model how to use glue, and don't make a sample collage. When teachers make a sample, children tend to want to make ones just like it. Three of our favorite collage ideas begin on page 21.

Getting Started

Put glue into a recycled plastic pint container with a foam brush or a tongue depressor. Also provide paper clips, tape, and a stapler to offer multiple ways to fasten materials together.

During collage making, use lots of rich vocabulary to discuss children's creations. When they say to you "Look what I did!" or "See what I made!" ask open-ended questions to encourage conversations about their work. You could post a list of questions and prompts in your art center to remind you what to ask (see "Questions to Ask Children About Collage" on p. 24).

Torn Paper Collage

This type of collage is the easiest for children to create.

1. Provide white glue and two different colors or types of paper (black and white construction paper work very well, or newspaper with black construction paper as a background).
2. Model tearing paper into unusual shapes. Encourage children to use a pincer grip with their fingertips.
3. Sing this tearing song to the tune of "Frere Jacques":

> Tearing, tearing
> Tearing, tearing
> 1, 2, 3
> 1, 2, 3
> What's it going to be now?
> What's it going to be now?
> Wait and see . . .
> Wait and see . . .

4. Demonstrate gluing one piece on the paper and holding it until it sticks.
5. Tear another shape and repeat. Ask some of the open-ended questions from the list on page 24.
6. Give children plenty of time to tear pieces of different sizes and shapes.
7. After children have torn plenty of paper, provide the glue. Give each child one page for attaching pieces.

Cut Paper Collage

For these collages, cut odd shapes of paper. Have the children cut the shapes if they can.

1. Model cutting and placing one or two pieces on the paper.
2. Discuss using unusual shapes (or cut these shapes) in addition to the geometric shapes the children know.
3. Sing the tearing song to the tune of "Frere Jacques" as with torn paper collage, but replace the word tearing with cutting.

3-D Collage

This activity is more appropriate for 4-year-olds than for most 3-year-olds.

1. Prepare strips of paper (for example, 1" x 6") before the activity.
2. Teach children to fold the ends of a strip into 1" "feet."
3. Show children how to glue the feet down and how they can make the papers jump over each other.
4. Heighten children's awareness of 3-D by placing small objects, such as toy cars, under the popped-up pieces. Talk about how things can go over, under, and around these shapes.
5. Children can also make pieces pop up by folding them in half and gluing down one half. As children master this technique, they can cut or tear other shapes to use in their pop-up collages, and attach these pieces to other popped-up pieces. This will be very exciting for them, and amazing works of art will spring off the page!

Display three-dimensional collages on a wall. Anything that falls off can be repaired at the "Art Hospital." You can put a child in charge of being the "Art Doctor" to make sure all the collages stay together.

Teacher: José, does your picture have a story?

José [referring to a book he read]: Yeah! The big guy is making lots of swords like in the movies and these little guys are gonna tell him to stop it. 'Cause like in the story you read us about the good dragon, they're gonna help the dragon find someone to play with.

Teacher: Oh, I'm so glad you are thinking about helping people while you make your collage. Are you planning to add some more curly shapes like the ones you already placed on your paper? Why?

Teacher: Liliana, what are you going to call that shape?

Liliana: It's all the twirly lines—and 1, 2, 3 kinds of them! I'm making lots and lots more to fill up all the paper! See, that one has a big hole in it.

Teacher: I wonder if you could figure out a way to make holes in some new shapes for your collage.

Teacher: Ashley, how did you get those shapes to pop up off your paper?

Ashley: I made a bridge like the George Washington Bridge that I went over with my grandma when we went to New York. I put the glue on the end and was bending it and holding it for a long time like in the glue song. See? And all these are the buildings in New York but some are in New Jersey. And I made a big fish going under the bridge.

Teacher: What other kinds of things do you remember from your trip over the bridge that you might add to your collage?

- How did you make that shape?
- What were you thinking about when you made that shape?
- What name do you want to give this shape?
- How can you attach your shape to the background paper without glue?
- Where on the page are you going to put it?
- How many pieces do you have so far? How many pieces do you think you'll use?
- Where do you think a second (third, fourth) piece should go?
- Should this shape touch the other shape?
- Should it go on top, or overlap the other shape?
- What do you see? What makes you say that?
- Which is the top (bottom) of the shape?
- What happens if you turn your collage upside-down?
- Will you make more shapes that are similar or will you make different shapes?
- What story does your picture tell?
- I see you have used _____ (curved, jagged, straight, etc.) lines in your collage. What other lines can you use?
- Are you planning to have any pieces stand up? How will you attach them?

Picture Books That Use Collage as Illustrations

Place inspirational books such as these in the art area.

- *Joseph Had a Little Overcoat*, by Simms Taback
- *It Looked Like Spilt Milk*, by Charles G. Shaw
- *Little Blue and Little Yellow*, by Leo Lionni
- *Nuts to You*, by Lois Ehlert
- *Perfect Square*, by Michael Hall
- *Snowballs*, by Lois Ehlert

- Good quality construction paper (This makes a difference. Try papers yourself to see how easy they are to tear, cut, and fold. You want the children to have a challenging but satisfying experience. If the paper is too thick, they will be frustrated.)
- Wallpaper samples
- Wrapping paper
- Brown paper bags
- Origami paper
- Tissue paper

Adaptations for Children With Special Needs

- Use papers with varied textures, such as wallpaper samples, copier paper, and crepe paper for children who have visual impairments.
- Use solid glue sticks instead of white glue.
- Plan large-scale group projects using colored butcher paper spread over a table.
- Provide a brief demonstration and organize the art materials at the tables ahead of time for children with attention challenges.
- Give each child his or her own supplies and plenty of elbow room.
- Use soft, soothing colors for children who might have emotional issues.
- Use larger paper for the bases for children with dexterity issues.

Use Just Enough Glue

Triada uses a rhyme to help children learn how to get just enough glue on a Popsicle stick, and then onto their paper pieces.

"Tap, tap, tap" is for tapping the Popsicle stick on the side of the container to get rid of some excess glue; "Wipe, wipe, wipe" reminds children to wipe the Popsicle stick on the side of the container to get rid of more excess; and "Spread, spread, spread / Like jelly on the bread" tells children to spread the glue onto the paper piece to be attached.

Books With Engaging Illustrations

Susan Friedman

Use diverse and compelling illustrations as a jumping-off point for classroom activities. You can inspire children to expand their use of different materials for art and to tell stories.

Pocketful of Posies: A Treasury of Nursery Rhymes, illustrated by Salley Mavor. 2010. Houghton Mifflin Books for Children.

Sixty-four rhymes spread over 64 pages include classics such as "Baa, Baa, Black Sheep," "Old King Cole," and "Jack and Jill," indexed for easy reference. Meticulously stitched fabric relief collages illustrate each rhyme. The fabrics are rich with texture, and Mavor adds detail with colorful stitching, buttons, bark, shells, and bells.

Last Night, by Hyewon Yum. 2008. Farrar Straus Giroux.

In this wordless book, linocut illustrations—prints made from carvings on blocks of linoleum—portray a girl who is sent to bed in a sour mood after refusing her dinner. When her teddy bear comes to life in her dreams, they embark on a fantastic adventure with animals in the forest nearby. Yum's layered prints, in hues muted and bright, capture the girl's range of emotions as her disappointing night becomes anything but.

In the Small, Small Pond, by Denise Fleming. 1993. Henry Holt.

With rhythm, rhyme, and alliteration, Fleming shows readers how much hustle and bustle is caused by the variety of animals in one small pond. Made from colored cotton pulp poured into hand-cut stencils, her bright and organic handmade-paper illustrations capture the energy of the geese, minnows, muskrats, and other animals.

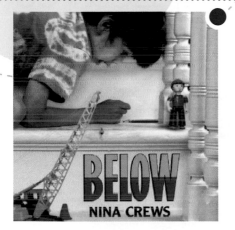

Below, by Nina Crews. 2006. Henry Holt.

The staircase in Jack's house serves as the backdrop for adventures with his action figure, Guy. Layered images of foliage, mountains, city streets, and dragons—a melding of photographs and some line drawings—transform pictures of their play into dramatic stories straight from Jack's imagination. When Guy falls into a small hole in one of the stairs, Jack's imagination and rescue skills kick into action.

Talk about the materials shown in the books. Children may spot the seashells, bells, or stitching that Mavor uses or see how Crews's illustrations include photographs. Do Yum's linocut illustrations remind children of stamps? Explain how Fleming uses colorful paper pulp to create her illustrations. What kinds of artwork do the children notice in their favorite books?

Make relief collages. Start with a base of paper or cloth, and invite children to layer on scraps and objects, such as magazine pictures and print, construction paper, newsprint, felt, cloth cut or torn into various shapes, buttons, and shells. In the fall, children can use leaves. Let them experiment with texture, shape, and color.

Make prints. Use tempera paint and materials like sponges cut into different shapes, feathers, shells, leaves, a potato masher, or the bottoms of old shoes. After the paint has dried, let children return to their work to add a second layer of color to transform their prints.

Tell stories with photographs. After reading *Below*, provide a selection of photos from magazines. Each child can choose three or four photos for inspiration to create a story. Include diverse people, places, and things in the collection of images. If a digital camera is available, children can pose items from the classroom and take photographs to tell their stories.

Collecting, Painting, and Studying Leaves

Jolyn Blank and Ellie Wastin

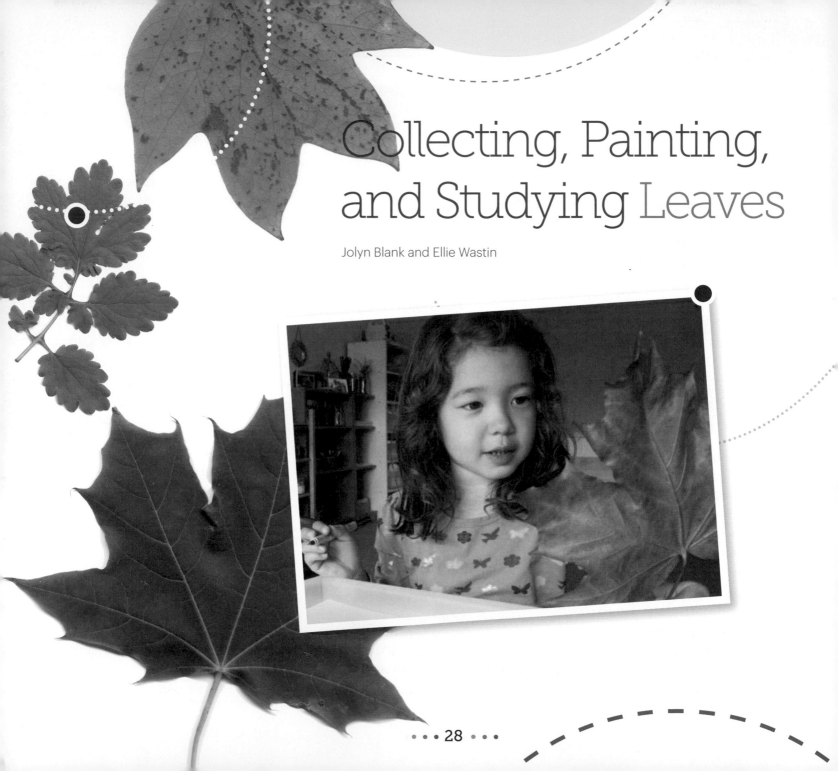

Why do this activity? In this activity, preschoolers can observe nature, collect fallen leaves, and use them to make art. Children plan how to use the leaves and use specific vocabulary to describe their creations. This activity supports many early learning standards for science, visual arts, language arts, and approaches to learning.

What can children learn? When preschoolers examine and compare natural objects, they begin to think like scientists. They develop their observation skills and explore natural objects with their senses. Children can also consider leaves' colors, sizes, shapes, textures, and weights when making their art.

Vocabulary words: *veins, chlorophyll, tree names, spring, summer, fall, winter, line, sharp, smooth, zigzag, curvy, shade, light, dark*

Materials:
- Paints (acrylic or other)
- Brushes
- Paper (we used clear acetate paper that displays well on windows)
- Leaves collected outdoors
- Smocks
- Easels and/or table coverings
- Magnifying lenses
- Books about trees
- Photographs of leaves, including close-up and magnified images

Prepare for the Activity

1. Collect leaves on a walk or in the playground, or ask children to bring them from home. Offer paint in the colors of the different leaves collected. Provide various shades of colors (for example, greens, yellows, and browns) in small cups.
2. Set up a space where children can work for an extended period of time, look at leaves and other natural objects, and choose to revisit work later. Make sure children can easily reach leaves and magnifying lenses and look closely as they paint.
3. Plan questions to ask children while they paint. Questions can incorporate the new vocabulary words and encourage children to focus on leaves, paint, and their general observations and work.

Lead Small Groups

1. Invite four to six children to participate.
2. Introduce the paint, brushes, and new vocabulary.
3. Demonstrate ways to use the brushes and paint to achieve various effects such as thick or fine lines, strong or sheer color, and texture. Challenge children to plan how they will use the leaves, either painting over them or incorporating them in another way.
4. Help children get started by posing questions like, "How will you start?" and "What kinds of lines can you make?" During painting, pose questions like, "How are the leaves the same or different?" and "What else do you see?" Give specific feedback or narrate the experience. For example, "I see you are making wavy lines," "I notice you are using light and dark green," or "These lines make me think of the veins of the leaf."
5. Give children plenty of time to carry out their plans.
6. Place finished artwork in a safe place to dry.

Respond to Individual Needs

1. Comment on and ask children questions about their work. Engage them in conversations. Encourage them to talk with others, exchange feedback, and think about what they want to do. Note that some children need time to explore using paintbrushes and the properties of the paint, particularly if they have not had much experience painting.
2. Use language that refers to the "here and now" (for example, real objects), which supports dual language learners. For example, say, "This leaf is green. Es verde," while holding a green leaf.

Follow Up After the Activity

Start a classroom collection of leaves and natural artifacts such as pine cones and acorns. Use the new vocabulary to describe the objects. Create a space where children can categorize and sort the items. Read and review fiction and nonfiction books about leaves and trees.

Involve Families

Create a guidebook about leaves that children can share with their families. Suggest that families go on neighborhood walks to find natural objects to add to the classroom collection. These can be actual items, such as fallen leaves, tree bark, and branches, or photographs of birds and squirrels that live in trees. Continue to sort and re-sort the items. Invite families to add information to the guidebook and then share these new entries with the children.

Splatter Paint

Violet McGillen

Why do this activity? Art experiences help promote children's healthy self-esteem. Children explore what appeals to them visually, learn how to appreciate their work and the work of the other children, and feel proud when they complete a project.

What can children learn? How to ask questions, follow rules, share supplies, and explore different materials and techniques. They can develop small motor skills and hand-eye coordination plus identify colors and shapes, develop spatial awareness, and explore their creativity.

Vocabulary words: *blend, splatter, splat, patterns, space*

Materials:
- Large cardboard box
- Packing tape
- Paintbrushes
- Tempera paint (3 or more colors)

Lead Small Groups

1. Give the instructions to two or three children who come to the splatter paint center, and provide a brief demonstration. Because of the nature of this activity, children must take turns. Children may watch a friend painting, discuss the experience, or work at a center nearby while waiting about five minutes for a turn.
2. Have the child who is about to paint put on a smock.
3. Write the child's name on a piece of white paper and place it name-side down in the bottom of the box.
4. Have the child dip the paintbrush into the paint, then splash and splatter it across the paper while kneeling by the box. He or she can switch brushes and repeat with another color.
5. When the artist finishes, lift the paper carefully, as it may be very wet. Put it on the newspaper-covered table until it dries enough to put on a drying rack overnight.

Respond to Individual Needs

1. Children with physical disabilities can stand instead of kneeling, but prepare for a larger splatter zone. Teachers can guide children who do not understand the process using a hand-over-hand method (the adult holds the child's hand while the child holds the paintbrush).
2. Introduce vocabulary words in English and in the children's home languages. Use the words to describe children's artwork.

Prepare for the Activity

1. Fold down the box flaps and secure them to the outside of the box with packing tape.
2. Designate an area of the room for the activity. Spread newspaper on the floor and table. Place the box on the floor on top of the newspaper, with the open side up.
3. Set out the paint on the table, along with a separate brush for each color.
4. Introduce Jackson Pollock during circle time by displaying photos of his works and of him painting. Talk about his techniques, including how he would stand above his canvas and splatter paint onto it with a brush. Tell the children they will have an opportunity to try splatter painting individually.

Follow Up After the Activity

1. Frame the dry paintings by mounting each on a large sheet of colored paper. Post them with a label showing the artist's name so children can see their own creations and those of their classmates.
2. Allow time for the children to observe and discuss their paintings together and with their families.
3. Place books about painting and artists in the literacy center.
4. Add an easel and an artist prop box to the dramatic play area. Include items like paintbrushes, sponges, blank canvasses, plastic fruit, postcards or posters of famous works of art, smocks, and so on.

Involve Families

1. Announce the activity in a family newsletter or on a bulletin board. Explain how to use a bucket of water and varied brushes outdoors to splatter water on sidewalks, driveways, and walls. Suggest that they discuss the shapes and patterns they create.
2. Take photos of the children doing the activity. Email them to families or post them on the program's website.

Talk With Children as They Paint

Hold individual conversations with children who are interested in discussing their painting process. Ask them about the patterns they see in their unique paintings and any images that emerge. Here are some ways to start the conversation:

1. Tell me about what you are doing.
2. What happens when you splatter the paint close to your paper? What happens when you splatter the paint from farther away?
3. Look at the paper. Which color do you want to use next so that you can fill the paper?
4. Which do you like best, large splotches or small drips?
5. When the colors blend, what new colors do you see?
6. What designs do you see in the splatter?

Discovering Science While Exploring Art

Sara Starbuck and Leigh Tyler Marshall-Oliver

When children use art materials, they make science discoveries. Adding water makes clay softer or paint thinner. You can use a glue stick to attach a scrap of paper, but it takes stronger glue to attach a pebble to a collage. To take advantage of these teachable moments and foster scientific inquiry, teachers can use some or all of the following five steps (National Research Council 1996) and the ideas on page 36.

1. Ask scientific questions

Use questions to spur children's thinking or make statements that start with "I wonder . . ."

- "I wonder if there is a way to make this paint a lighter color."
- "I wonder why this clay is soft and that clay is hard."
- "What do you think will happen if you move the bottle around while you squirt the paint?"

2. **Encourage investigating through exploration**
   - Provide a wide variety of materials.
   - Offer choices and allow plenty of time for children to explore the materials.
   - Focus on the process of art, not the finished product.
   - Encourage observation and attention to detail.
   - Model observation:

     "I notice that this part of the clay feels smooth and the rest is bumpy."

     "I see that each petal of the sunflower has a pointed tip."

     "I notice that when you push on the stick, it makes dents in the clay."

3. **Gather and record data**

   When children explore, they learn new facts and information—what scientists call data. Teach children how to present the data in drawings and simple charts.

4. **Use data to construct reasonable explanations**

   Help children examine the data and come up with possible explanations. Some conclusions may be mistaken, but children can continue to gather data and adjust their hypotheses over time.
   - "What did you notice about the paints when you mixed them?"
   - "What happened when you added white?"
   - "Which colors are stronger [overpowering other colors] and which are weaker [easily overpowered]?"

5. **Communicate discoveries**

   Like scientists, children can share and discuss their work with others. Help children record their data and explanations in a journal. Teachers can create posters for the classroom, post dictation next to children's art, and make documentation displays using photographs, drawings, and writing.

Introduce New Words

Introduce vocabulary that enhances children's language and thinking skills.

- "Purple is made up of red and blue. It is a *secondary color*."
- "The clay is *dense*. You have to push it really hard with the rolling pin to make it flat."
- "Notice how some colors are bright and some colors are pale. We call the pale colors *pastels*."

Provide Encouragement and Feedback

Recognize small accomplishments and help children notice the details of their work.

- "I notice that you worked hard to balance that piece of wood on your sculpture."
- "You filled your whole paper with dots. Some are big and some are tiny."
- "I see you used water to make the clay softer. That solved your problem."

Explain the Reasoning Behind Actions

Children learn more and can apply their knowledge in new situations when you explain why they might want to do something.

- "If you tap your brush gently on the edge of the paint cup, the paint won't drip when you put the brush on the paper."
- "When you want the paint to be lighter, adding the white paint works best because it is the lightest."
- "When the clay is dry, it is hard to work. When you add water, the clay absorbs the water and becomes softer."

Promote Further Exploration

Ask simple questions to challenge children to investigate more.

- "I notice that when you hold the dropper still, the paint pools underneath. What do you think would happen if you moved the dropper around?"
- "What happens when you hold the dropper high? How about when you hold it low? Why do you think that happens?"

Experiment With Temporary Art

Many artists work in temporary media. When children explore the properties of light and shadows while playing with a projector or a light table, a teacher can point out science concepts and introduce vocabulary.

- "When you block the light with your body, you make a shadow on the wall."
- "When you put an object on the projector, it stops or absorbs the light."

Supporting Dual Language Learners

What sets these science discoveries apart from simply messing around with art materials is the talk, which may not reach children who are new to English. Teachers can support science inquiry for dual language learners by preparing adaptations in advance.

- Learn to say "I wonder" and key science and art phrases in the languages of your classroom.
- Use visuals such as modeling, pictures, and rebus messages to convey the steps in the scientific process.
- Take time with individual children who need more help to understand.
- Invite bilingual parents, older students, or community volunteers to be visiting scientists.

REFERENCE

National Research Council. 1996. *National Science Education Standards: Observe, Interact, Learn, Change*. Washington, DC: National Academies Press. www.nap.edu/openbook.php?record_id=4962.

Art Learning Center Checklist

Laura J. Colker

You can complete this checklist for the art learning center in your classroom on your own, or with a teaching colleague. When you are finished, review the items you rated as "rarely" and create an action plan to help change the rating to "sometimes" or "regularly."

	Regularly	Sometimes	Rarely
1. Children choose to play in the art center every day.	○	○	○
2. Children know and follow the rules for using the art center.	○	○	○
3. The center is located near a water source for mixing paints and cleaning up.	○	○	○
4. Materials are stored in labeled containers and shelves within children's reach.	○	○	○
5. There are books about artists and art techniques.	○	○	○
6. Children can save their creations and work on them later.	○	○	○
7. Children have fun and express pleasure in creating art.	○	○	○
8. While using the art center, children express thoughts and feelings and build skills in all domains.	○	○	○
9. The art center has			
• Materials for drawing, painting (including at least one easel), sculpting and molding, and constructing	○	○	○
• Places for drying artwork	○	○	○
• A table where children can work on projects	○	○	○
• Smocks and shirts to protect children's clothing	○	○	○
• Children's artwork, which is framed and hung at children's eye level	○	○	○
10. Teachers extend children's play by			
• Engaging children in conversations	○	○	○
• Asking questions	○	○	○
• Responding to children's questions	○	○	○
• Offering ideas	○	○	○
• Commenting on children's explorations and creations	○	○	○
• Providing new props that offer different experiences and challenges	○	○	○

Music and
Movement

The Power of Creative Dance

Connie Bergstein Dow

Peek into my creative dance class where a teacher and preschoolers sway from side to side. We are imagining ourselves on a boat trip, visiting exotic destinations. Or see us creeping through the jungle, spotting different animals. We move like each animal we encounter—swimming, crawling, galloping, and soaring.

Moving is one of the most important ways preschoolers explore and learn about the world, and this process continues as they develop. Creative movement is an important part of every early childhood curriculum. Guided creative movement helps children understand concepts kinesthetically (through the body). Movement activities also help children learn to control their bodies, follow instructions, listen for cues, and respect others in a shared space—all skills that they will use in kindergarten.

What Is Creative Movement?

The terms *dance* and *movement* are interchangeable when referring to creative movement. Creative movement is an art form whose medium is the human body in motion. The four basic elements of dance are the body and its range of movement, space, time, and energy. Teachers can use these four elements to create endless movement possibilities.

For example, enliven marching—a basic locomotor movement—by varying the four elements:

Body: "Can you march with your arms up high?" "Can you march on your tiptoes? Lying on your back with your feet in the air?"

Space: "Can you march backward? Low? High?" "Can you march in a square pattern?"

Time: "Can you march in slow motion?" "March for seven steps and freeze. Let's count together."

Energy: "Can you march like you are in quicksand?" "Can you march like you are barefoot on a hot sidewalk?"

Children can perform variations according to their individual abilities and imaginations. Creative movement teaches children that there can be many solutions to a question, problem, or task.

Benefits of Creative Movement

Dance can powerfully impact children's daily lives. Here are some ways to invite all children to dance.

Provide Access for All

Movement activities require little equipment. The ideal space, such as a gym, is clear of obstacles and well defined. However, teachers can adapt activities to smaller, irregular spaces that do have obstacles. In these situations, choose activities that children can do in place, such as learning about opposites: "While staying in your spot, can you show me the opposites, high and low? Straight and crooked? Tired and energetic?" Later, incorporate the obstacles: "Let's march around the bookcase!"

Use a small drum, tambourine, or other device to give auditory cues. A flashlight can be a tool for giving visual cues. Use a CD or MP3 player to provide lively musical accompaniment.

Teachers can adapt movement activities so all children can participate. For example, in a greeting activity that involves waving body parts, children with physical disabilities can move their tongues, eyelids, or toes. A jumping activity can include children in wheelchairs who can move their heads, arms, or fingers. In an alphabet game where children form letters with their bodies, children with special needs can use part of the body or point to a picture of the letter. Dance stories let children of all abilities respond to literature through movement. (See "Dance Stories," p. 62.)

Enrich the Curriculum

Use movement sessions to integrate physical activities with other areas of the curriculum and all learning domains—physical, social and emotional, and cognitive. Movement works well as a teaching strategy for themes, such as animals, plants, and transportation. It also can address early learning standards. Here are examples.

Invite children to use their bodies to form shapes, walk in floor patterns such as figure eights and zigzag lines, or jump and make shapes in the air, like an X or Y. While playing a dance/freeze game, children can dance freely until the teacher stops the music and gives instructions: "Freeze in a twisty shape!" "Freeze in a wide shape!"

Integrate movement into a learning game when children are fidgety. A teacher might say, "Let's count to five while we fidget." Fidgeting can become a vocabulary game: "What is another word for fidget? Squirm! Jiggle! Wiggle!"

Promote Physical Development

Through creative movement activities, children learn body control. They become aware of how to stop and start, and how to change speed and direction. They also learn spatial concepts and respect for personal space. These lessons carry over into children's other activities and behavior.

Guided creative movement helps young children learn new motor skills and practice those they know. Preschoolers love expansive movements and enjoy practicing large motor skills such as walking, galloping, tiptoeing, hopping, jumping, and turning. As children repeat and change basic motor skills, they improve their coordination, balance, stamina, and strength.

Encourage Social and Emotional Development

Creative movement works well as a group activity and fosters cooperation. A teacher can suggest movements for children to do on their own or with a partner. "How many ways can you move from sitting to standing?" and group activities: "Imagine we are back in the days of the dinosaurs. Can you move like a pterodactyl?"

Movements that involve more than one child help preschoolers learn to work together and value individual contributions. Listening and responding to directions, offering suggestions, exploring others' ideas while waiting for a turn, and moving together are opportunities for learning and practicing social skills.

Children can also mature psychologically and emotionally by using movement for self-expression. Dance can be an outlet for the emotions of children who cannot express themselves verbally.

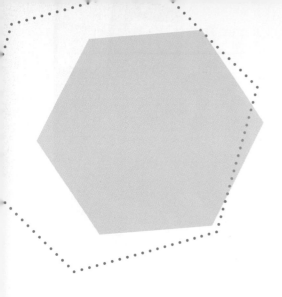

Support Creative Thinking

To prepare children for the future, we need to teach them to look at problems in new ways, practice critical thinking skills, and collaborate to find solutions. A strong workforce will rely on creative thinkers who can see patterns and innovations.

The creative arts nurture these aspects of developing children. Movement allows young children to approach tasks through the body and come up with new questions and new answers.

Movement and exercise can spark the growth of new brain cells and facilitate learning (Ratey 2008). In his book *Spark: The Revolutionary New Science of Exercise and the Brain,* John J. Ratey notes that exercise prepares the brain to capture new information.

Creative dance is the perfect vehicle for enhancing the mind-body connection in young children. Once educators become familiar with movement and its many benefits, instead of asking, "What is creative movement?" the question will be, "Why not creative movement?"

Greetings

"Let's wave to each other with our hands. What other parts of your body can you wave? Can you wave all the parts at once?"

Themes

Add movement to any topic the children are exploring. For example, prompt children to create a gardening dance: dig holes, plant seeds, water, weed, and harvest the flowers.

Transitions

"Today let's explore how animals move. Think of your favorite animal. I am going to ask you one by one to move like that animal as you go to your cubby." Use cues for signaling the start and stop for each child's movement. For several days, continue this activity during transitions. Narrow the choices each day: flying animals, ocean animals, jungle animals.

Props

Provide scarves, streamers, shakers, costumes, small musical instruments, flashlights or fiber-optic lights, stuffed animals, pom-poms, hats, and any items the children make. Invite children to dance using their props.

Quiet-Down Activities

Bring each activity to a quiet conclusion. You could ask the children to freeze in a shape (connected to the theme) at the end of a dancing session. For example, to finish an activity about winter, prompt: "Can you freeze in the shape of a snowflake? Try to hold that shape as you melt to the floor!"

Group Time

"Do you know the game Telephone? You whisper a word in your neighbor's ear, and she whispers it to the next person. This movement game is like that, except we pass along movements. I will think of the first one."

Begin with something simple, like crossing and uncrossing your arms. The next person watches, turns to his neighbor, and performs the same movement. Children pass it along until it goes all the way around the circle. Repeat until everyone has introduced a movement.

At the end, review all the movements together, in order. Add music, and the movements become a dance!

REFERENCE

Ratey, J.J. 2008. *Spark: The Revolutionary New Science of Exercise and the Brain*. New York: Little, Brown.

Music and Movement Learning Center

Laura J. Colker

What Children Do and Learn

Math

- Notice a pattern when they clap or stomp to the beat of the music.
- Hold notes while singing for differing lengths of time/number of beats.
- Hang instruments on peg board on top of paper shapes.

Language and Literacy

- Learn music terminology in English and home languages: *tempo, rhythm, pitch, melody.*
- Return music and instruments to the shelves labeled with the appropriate pictures and words.
- Read aloud books based on songs, such as *The Wheels on the Bus, Sing,* and *There Was an Old Lady Who Swallowed a Fly.*

Physical

- Learn to play a kazoo.
- Move to music like a giraffe or other animals.
- Do a musical finger play.

Creativity

- Sing, listen to music, play instruments, and move to music.
- Draw or dance to music.
- Learn dances from different countries.

Social and Emotional

- Discuss how music or movement makes them feel.
- Express feelings with their hands, their feet, or their whole bodies.

Setup Tips

- Select a large, open area where children can move in different ways. Since children are bound to be boisterous at times, locate the center away from quiet areas such as the literacy center.
- Provide carpeting so children can sit or stretch out on the floor and listen to music with headphones.
- Include storage space for music, instruments, and movement props.
- Take the instruments and movement props outside so children can enjoy a loud march or run and twirl to lively music.

Budget Stretchers

- Make musical instruments with the children. Several Internet sites provide how-to information (for example, www.busybeek idscrafts.com/Homemade-Musical-Instru ments.html). Also, see "A Place for Making Instruments" on page 50.
- Search for inexpensive or free music of every genre on Internet sites that follow copyright laws. Make CDs or DVDs or download music to a tablet, computer, or MP3 player.
- Provide inexpensive or donated scarves or pieces of fabric for children to use as props while moving and dancing.

Beyond the Basics

- Think of music as a form of communication. Preschoolers can learn to read and write music just as they learn English or a second language. Introduce basic symbols and notation.
- Teach music and dance appreciation by helping children pay attention to and talk about what they like about a particular instrument, dance style, or song.

Include Children's Families and Cultures

- Include books, signs, and labels in both English and children's home languages.
- Offer the kinds of music and movement that children enjoy at home.
- Encourage visiting family members to introduce children to a song, an instrument, or a dance that represents their cultures.

A Place for Making Musical Instruments

Laura J. Colker

Making instruments allows children to follow directions, add their own creative touches, and play with sounds. After making instruments, children can use them to express themselves through music on their own and with classmates.

Materials—Children can use many different kinds of materials to make musical instruments. Some possibilities include string, rubber bands, tissue boxes, plastic wrap, paper plates, cardboard rolls, paints, Popsicle sticks, markers, and tape. Teachers may also want to keep the center stocked with books about music and musical instruments, trays so that children can easily transport their work, and picture instructions for simple musical instruments.

Instruments

- **Paper plate tambourines:** Pour beads or buttons onto a paper plate. Fold the plate in half. Punch holes along the sides of the plate and tie together with colorful string to keep the tambourine together. Children can also seal the ends with tape or glue.
- **Hand-clappers:** Trace hands on cardboard or sturdy paper and cut them out. Glue each hand onto a Popsicle stick. Hold the two hands together and shake them to make a clapping sound. Children may also enjoy decorating the instruments with paints, markers, and crayons.
- **Tissue-box guitars:** Wrap rubber bands around an empty tissue box lengthwise. Glue or tape a cardboard tube on one end of the box, to serve as the handle. Children can strum the guitar by plucking the rubber bands.

What Children Do and Learn

Math

- Tie one bell through each punched hole in a paper plate tambourine.
- Use a paper plate as a template to make a waxed paper circle to cover the end of a paper-towel-roll kazoo.
- Select two Popsicle sticks and two juice lids to make hand clappers.

Language and Literacy

- Follow picture and word directions to create instruments.
- Look at books about musical instruments.
- Return supplies to labeled storage areas.

Physical

- Wrap rubber bands around an open container to make a kalimba.
- Punch holes in canvas for lacing a drum.
- Decorate instruments with paint, markers, and crayons.

Setup Tips

- Provide a table and floor space where children can work undisturbed.
- Use trays to carry supplies from the art center (paint, brushes, markers, glue, scissors, glitter) and the cooking center (plastic wrap, waxed paper) for children's use in making and decorating instruments.
- Store loose items such as fabric scraps, ribbon, twist ties, and rubber bands in open containers.

Budget Stretchers

- Ask families to donate music-making materials found around the home: rubber bands, twist ties, tin cans (be sure to smooth rough edges), empty oatmeal boxes, food storage containers, and the like.
- Collect and use recyclables: fabric scraps, paper towel rolls, cardboard boxes, and so on.
- Check out yard sales and dollar stores for instruments and items children can use to make instruments.

Include Children's Families and Cultures

- Ask families to share examples of musical instruments from their cultures to inspire children to make similar ones. Find photos on the Internet to show children instruments that are new to them.
- Request that families loan the class music (CDs or other recordings) featuring instruments special to their cultures. This will guide children in learning to play these instruments.
- Send home instructions and materials for making simple musical instruments. Families and children can create and then enjoy these instruments at home.

Promoting Music Play

Kristen M. Kemple, Jacqueline J. Batey, and Lynn C. Hartle

Is music part of your curriculum? Playing with music, like playing with blocks, painting, and pretending, is a chance for children to learn about themselves, others, and the world. Music play is fun. And it may open the door to a child's lifelong interest in and love of music.

Here are some ways to encourage preschoolers to play with music.

1 **Provide a variety of drums and strikers.**
Children will discover through trial and error as they play with sounds. "I make one sound when I hit this little drum and another sound when I hit this big one." You support their play when you expect and allow for noise.

2 **Play a variety of music in your classroom and outdoors.**
Introduce different styles of music—jazz, classical, popular, ragtime, folk, and music from around the world, such as Argentinean tangos, Indian sitar melodies, Zimbabwean mbira, Celtic lullabies, and Slovakian polkas.

3 Offer props that encourage children to move to music in different ways.

Provide scarves, streamers, hula hoops, and pool noodles. Share children's joy and delight in their fun.

4 Teach children songs and sing often.

Invent new words for familiar songs. For example, to the tune of "The Farmer in the Dell," sing, "We're cleaning up our room, we're cleaning up our room. We're putting all the blocks away, we're cleaning up our room." Invite children to create new songs.

5 Invite musicians to visit the program.

Music students, teachers, family members, and professionals can talk about their instrument and how they play them. Children can gently strum a guitar, blow through a piccolo, or experiment with the sounds different mallets make on a steel drum.

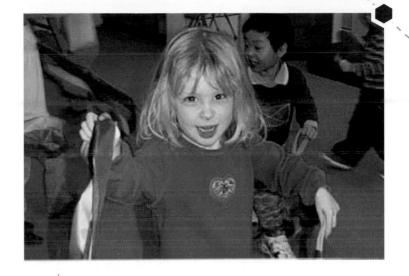

6 Create a music center that offers musical options during choice time.

Stock the center with interesting things that invite children to explore sounds and make music in their own unique ways.

7 Join in.

Can't carry a tune? No problem. Do you let the fact that you are not an artist keep you from giving children markers and paints to explore? There are many ways you can make sure children have lots of music in their lives.

8 Read and discuss music-related books.

This Jazz Man, by Karen Ehrhardt, introduces nine of the world's greatest jazz players. Children can play and sing along as the text features lyrics to go with familiar tunes.

A Stage for the Playground: An Outdoor Music Center

Carol Garboden Murray

Building a stage on your playground is a wonderful way to extend classroom learning to the outdoors. We built a beautiful cedar stage in a corner of our playground and created a music center.

We read *Max Found Two Sticks*, by Brian Pinkney, and learned that there are many ways to make music and rhythm.

Families helped us gather interesting items that we used to invent rhythm instruments to take outside. We put a big box in our entryway and collected coffee cans, hubcaps, pots and pans, cooking spoons, and all sorts of recycled items.

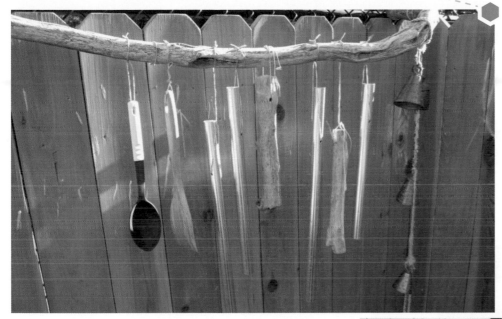

The children made their own drumsticks from wooden spoons purchased at the dollar store.

We integrated drums and music making into our curriculum. A musician, Uncle Rock, played music with us on our new stage. Everyone celebrated music and played our drums.

We collected chimes, bells, spoons, and driftwood and hung them in the corner of the stage. Then, the children experimented with the homemade hanging chimes and danced and jumped on our new stage.

We focused on making drums and found lots of different ways to make them. Some ideas were very simple—like turning over galvanized metal cans and plastic buckets to try out different types of sounds.

Drums come in different sizes. Coffee cans become little drums. We really enjoyed decorating them with colored tape!

We made big drums with construction tubes purchased at the hardware store. We covered these with gesso (a thin substance that primes the surface for painting) and then let the children paint them.

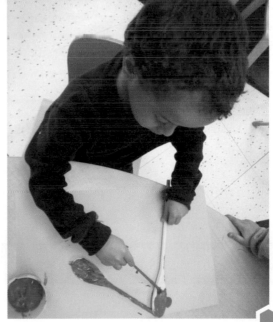

What We Learned

1. Playing drums outdoors is particularly enjoyable because it allows a great deal of freedom. Letting children experiment with rhythm is important, but it is often difficult to do indoors. Drums can be overwhelming (noisy) in the classroom. Our playground absorbs sound nicely, and children are free to explore both loud and quiet sounds and wild and controlled rhythms.

2. The stage itself creates a special sense of place. It inspires expression through dancing, singing, and acting out stories. Children behave differently when they step on the stage and become performers. The stage creates opportunities both to perform and to be an audience.

3. The playground is an extension of the classroom. We are excited about the potential that exists for integrating art, music, and creative expression into our outdoor play.

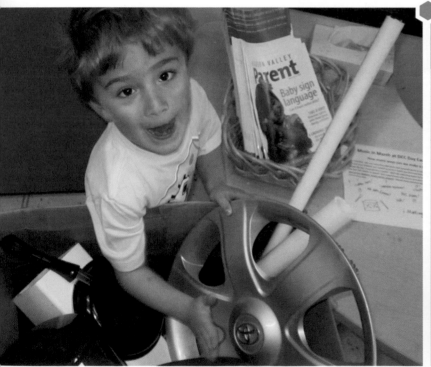

The author would like to thank New York State AEYC for awarding the mini grant that funded this project. www.nysaeyc.org/grant/minigrant.asp

Learning in Motion

Donna Furmanek

Movement activities for preschoolers can help them develop a lifelong love of movement. Teachers can plan movement so children can explore a wide range of motion and freedom of expression. Here are some ways to incorporate movement in the preschool day.

Being Aware of Oneself in Space

First, show preschoolers how to draw imaginary bubbles around their bodies. Encourage them to move in different ways within their bubbles. Children can pretend the bubble is shrinking and curl up small, pretend the bubble is growing and reach wide, or create a bubble dance.

Moving With the Beat

When preschoolers transition from one kind of activity to another, help them refocus with a steady, even beat. Tap your knees and invite children to join you. As you tap, say, "Beat, beat," to help them recognize the rhythm.

Moving With Objects

Fill a basket with props such as scarves, pieces of ribbon, or newspaper. These materials make different sounds, depending on how preschoolers move them.

Play some flowing or rhythmic music that inspires children to move freely using their props.

Experimenting With a Variety of Movements

Here are some ways preschoolers can explore different kinds of movement.

- **Punch:** Encourage children to pound, punch, and create with clay or dough.
- **Glide:** Provide finger paint to let children experience a gliding effect.
- **Slash:** Provide large sheets of newspaper for ripping and crepe paper or scarves for waving.
- **Dab:** Encourage children to dab on paint with sponges, bingo dabbers, or their fingers.
- **Wring:** Place large sponges at the water table for children to wring, or doll clothing to wash and wring.
- **Press:** Offer a variety of writing tools—crayons, markers, pencils, and chalk—so children can experience pressing to make a mark.

Moving throughout the day supports most areas of learning and development. Moving can keep preschoolers engaged and encourage their creativity. Have fun and keep it light. Let your own joy of movement come out.

Books That Feature Song Lyrics

Lauren Baker

Invite children to sing along with these books during your next read-aloud. Soon they'll be singing songs all through the day.

The Wheels on the Bus, adapted and illustrated by Paul O. Zelinsky. 1990. Dutton.

Many children are familiar with this classic song. Lively and interesting illustrations invite children to investigate the action in a small community. Interactive features, such as pull tabs and flaps, narrate the story. Since these features make the book fairly delicate, you may want to supervise or tape down the flaps when providing the book for younger preschoolers to explore.

Sing, lyrics and music by Joe Raposo. Illustrated by Tom Lichtenheld. 2013. Henry Holt.

This *Sesame Street* song is so familiar it may be hard to read aloud without everyone singing along. *Sing* comes with a recording of the song that children can listen to while looking at the book. The back pages include prints of the original hand-written chords and lyrics.

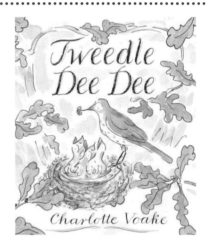

Tweedle Dee Dee, by Charlotte Voake. 2008. Candlewick.

This story is based on the traditional song "The Green Leaves Grew All Around." Two young children interact with nature, observe animals, and tenderly learn to appreciate the world around them.

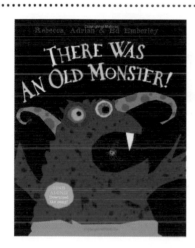

There Was an Old Monster!,
by Rebecca, Adrian, and Ed Emberley. 2009. Scholastic.

This silly variation on "There Was an Old Lady Who Swallowed a Fly" follows a monster as he swallows different creatures. Fun, bright cutouts allow us to see inside the monster's stomach as he eats.

Compose music. Books that are also songs often include music for and notes about the song. Encourage children to make up their own songs. They can record them in the music center using a tablet, computer, or tape recorder. Provide pencils and paper so children can jot down their ideas through drawing or imaginative writing.

Introduce patterns. Many songs incorporate patterns into their structure. They may begin or end each line with the same phrase, like in *The Wheels on the Bus* and *Tweedle Dee Dee*, or they may always come back to the same phrase or chorus, as in *Sing*. Using the books as examples, talk to the children about patterns. Then ask them if they can think of other patterns in the world around them (a consistent daily schedule is a good example). Encourage children to draw or create their own patterns from objects in the classroom.

Be inspired by the books. Invite children to illustrate a line from their favorite song. They can interpret it any way they like. After they have finished, write down the line that they say they have illustrated. Compile the drawings in a book and put it in the literacy center.

Dance Stories

Connie Bergstein Dow

Why do this activity? Descriptions of movement abound in children's literature. When preschoolers retell a story through dance, they can use their creativity and build their language and literacy skills.

What can children learn? Creating dance stories helps preschoolers learn about sequencing, identify with characters, understand the setting, acquire vocabulary, reinforce concepts from the stories, and gain many other valuable skills, including individual and group problem-solving, and body and spatial awareness.

Vocabulary words: music- and movement-related words such as *tiptoe, gallop, soar, swing, shuffle, sway, prance, twirl, tempo, rhythm,* and *percussion.* Also, new, interesting words from the stories.

Materials:

- Books (for example, consider *The Snowy Day*, by Ezra Jack Keats, or *Kitten's First Full Moon*, by Kevin Henkes)
- Music that goes well with the story
- DVD, MP3 player, or other equipment for playing music
- Props for dancing and acting out the story

Prepare for the Activity

1. Select five to seven elements in a book (or song, poem, or story) that could spark and prompt movement ideas, such as descriptions of a character or action pictures and words.
2. Choose music for the dance story. Look for a quiet instrumental piece, and intersperse a more upbeat song during active parts of the story.
3. Identify an open, unobstructed space for the dance story. Or, have children do the dance story in place.
4. Prepare the props you selected for the dance story. Enhance the activity by using props the children make ahead of time, such as shakers, streamers, and scarves, or colorful, decorated fabric.

Lead Small Groups

1. Split the class in half so no more than 10 to 12 children participate at a time.
2. Ask the audience to do something specific while they are watching the dancers. For example, invite them to look for people who are ice skating, building a snowman, or making footprints in the snow.
3. Read the book aloud to the class. Then ask the children to go to a personal space. Before you begin reading again, remind the children to be aware of others in the shared space around them.
4. Play the music. Retell the highlights of the story in the order they happen (using the five to seven elements you chose already), and call out movement prompts.
5. Observe children naturally thinking of variations as they relive the story through movement. Pick up on these, and add your own ideas, so that each part of the story is fully explored.
6. Move on to the next movement prompt until all are explored.
7. Conclude the story. Ask the children to hold a final position, come together in a circle, or return to their original spots. Alternatively, play an upbeat musical selection one more time and invite the children to dance about any of their new ideas about the story.

Respond to Individual Needs

1. Encourage all children to make their own movement choices. If a child has a limited range of movement, note how she responds within that range, while inviting her to discover different ways of moving.
2. Include a child who is not mobile by asking him to hold a prop and respond to the music. He can also help call out the prompts and hold the book, turn the pages, and show the illustrations sequentially.

Follow Up After the Activity

1. Have a follow-up discussion about the story or children's movement experiences.
2. Ask questions to reinforce learning and gain ideas for future activities:
   - What was your favorite part of the story to dance about? Why? Did it help you to move in a way that you have never tried before?
   - Which character(s) inspired you to dance? Did dancing help you to better understand that character(s) in the story?
   - Did you discover any fun new ways of moving by watching the other children as they danced about the story?
   - What other books, stories, or poems do you think we should use for a dance story? What props should we use?
   - What music would you like to use for a new dance story?

Involve Families

1. Ask families to help their children choose a favorite book (and music) to bring to the program to use for dance stories. At home, children can show their parents how they danced along with their special book.
2. Plan a dance story that involves something the children can bring from home, such as a story about animals. Ask the children to bring in a stuffed animal for the dance.
3. Plan an informal dance story session at an open house or family night at the program. Involve children and families in creating the dance story. Pose questions to the children and to their parents.

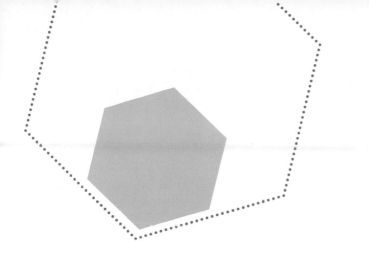

Attend a Live Performance

Susan Friedman

Why do this activity? Attending a live performance can be a wonderful way to introduce children to the performing arts. Many dance, music, and theater companies offer shows specifically geared to young children and their families. Attending high school or college music and drama productions is another way to introduce young children to live performance.

What can children learn? Attending live performances gives preschoolers an opportunity to gain an appreciation for dance, music, and drama. Follow-up discussions can inspire children to reenact the experience and plan their own performances.

Vocabulary words: any words related to the performance genre such as *character, ballet, oboe, puppeteer*

Materials:

- Camera
- Props
- Books
- Dress-up clothes
- Photographs
- Puppets
- Instruments
- Other items related to the performance

Prepare for the Activity

1. Call the theater in advance and ask what age children will enjoy the performance and how long the performance will last.
2. Explain to the children what you will see and hear during the performance. Discuss the characters, tell the story, or listen to other music in the same style. If the performance is based on a storybook, read it aloud several times.
3. Review appropriate audience manners. Remind the children of how to behave among large groups, out in public, and during quiet times. Explain when applause is appropriate and how to be courteous to other people attending the performance. Have the children practice for a few days.
4. Begin taking photos that document the activity from start to finish.

Lead Small Groups

1. Divide the children into small groups led by a teacher or other adult volunteer.
2. Arrive early so there is plenty of time to explore the theater. You might take a close-up look at the stage or peer into the orchestra pit. An early arrival also leaves plenty of time to use the restrooms and find your seats.
3. Recognize that it is okay to leave before the end of the performance. Preschoolers may find even a half-hour event too long. One teacher can take the children who have reached their limits to the lobby or outdoors to play a game or read a story. Another teacher can stay with the children who are still enjoying the show.

Respond to Individual Needs

1. Talk with a preschooler about what you saw and heard. Ask, "What did you think?" "What did you like best?" "How did you feel?"
2. Respond to special interests. Read a related book (for example, *Charlie Parker Played Be Bop*, by Chris Raschka, for a child who loves the saxophone), or do an art, music, or dance project that you know particular children will enjoy.

Follow Up After the Activity

Use the photos to recreate the experience. Make a book to place in the literacy center or a documentation panel to hang in the classroom. Talk with children about the event: What did we do first? Then what happened? "Which characters were your favorites?"

Involve Families

1. Share the photos you took with children's families by posting them outside the classroom door or through the classroom website or newsletter. Include quotes that express children's responses to the performance: "The orchestra was in a hole in front of the stage." "The actors wear lots of makeup." "I liked the big drum. It's called a timpani."
2. Ask families to share recordings of music they enjoy or that reflects their cultures. Invite parents who are musicians to visit the classroom to play for the children and talk about their instruments.

Supporting Dual Language Learners

Help dual language learners enjoy a live performance by providing a simple, visual orientation about what to expect from the experience. All children will be better prepared if they see a video clip of the performance or learn some of the music. Assign an adult to each child who is not fluent in English to keep children safe. Also give each child an identification card, tag, or bracelet in case the child gets separated from the group. For best results, use role-playing or video examples to show the children how to behave appropriately at the venue. This will help all of the children be confident about attending a live performance.

Learn, Sing, Play: Nature-Related, Low-Cost Music Activities

Petra Kern and Beth McLaughlin

Music is a unique tool for helping children develop skills in all developmental domains. Rethinking the way we use music in preschool settings and being creative in using available resources can support children's learning.

Music activities are motivating and engage children with various ability levels equally. They can be easily embedded in daily routines or adapted to individual needs. Today many early childhood programs face financial strains and must accomplish more with limited resources. Here are some examples of music activities that use natural and low-cost materials.

We hope you will be inspired to use these activities with preschoolers. When thinking creatively and following children's curiosity and imagination, you may discover many ways to help children appreciate nature and foster their learning while enjoying music.

Take a Soundwalk

What? A soundwalk is a method proposed by Canadian composer R. Murray Schafer for identifying a soundscape—the sounds typically heard—for a specific location (see Schafer 1993). Children and teachers walk through a natural area with their ears as open as possible.

Why? Children learn through listening, imitation, and repetition. A soundwalk will teach children focused listening, which is attentive and purposeful listening to the specific sounds in a chosen environment. Children learn about the nature and discuss how to preserve it.

How? Choose a nearby environment (ideally a place like a park). Or, just go outdoors and listen to the sounds of nature.

- Walk or take children on a field trip to the chosen location.
- Ask children to put on their listening ears and pay attention to all of the sounds they can hear around them.
- Invite children to share what they have heard and help them label the sounds correctly. If possible, let children touch, smell, and see the sound sources. If children hear a bird cooing, suggest looking up in a tree or on a rooftop to find the bird.
- Teach children something about what they have heard (the name of the bird and where it makes its nest).
- Ask children to use their voices to imitate the sounds. Lead them in using keynote sounds, figure sounds, and soundmarks.

Keynote sounds are environmental sounds that are steady, predictable, and always there (for example, the chirping of crickets). Figure sounds are surprising, sudden, or annoying (for example, a crow's cry or a camera click). Soundmarks are heard in reference to a specific place (for example, sirens in a city).

Extension. Record a soundwalk and bring it to the classroom. Let children guess where you recorded the sounds. Use props to illustrate the sound sources.

Read and discuss books about caring for the natural environment.

"It Looks Like Rain" Paddle Drum Activity

What? Explore ways to maximize the function of musical instruments available in your classroom. Paddle drums have a round, flat head attached to a handle. The head is pretuned. They come in different sizes. The larger the head, the deeper the sound.

In this activity, children can

- Hold and play the drum with a hand, a mallet, or other item
- Tickle, rub, tap, or hit the drum for different sound effects
- Play the paddle drum against different body parts
- Tie scarves to the handle and use the drum as a movement prop

Why? Playing the game "It Looks Like Rain" encourages children to explore sounds and move their bodies to music. Such games also help build children's language comprehension, improve fine motor skills, and increase spatial awareness. While playing the paddle drum, children can go from quiet to loud and slow to fast at specific points in a story; rub, tap, and hit the paddle drum using various hand and finger positions; and follow positional changes (for example, up and down) with the paddle drum.

How? Gather paddle drums, scarves or wrist streamers, and small laminated pictures of the sun.

Attach a scarf or wrist streamer to each paddle drum handle. Tape a picture of the sun to each paddle drum.

Have children sit in a circle, listen to the story, and follow your directions for what to do with their paddle drums.

Extensions. Add other sound effects (for example, a thunder tube to imitate the thunder, a rain stick to imitate the rain, or a gong to imitate the storm) and have children play them when cued.

Use any available hand drum or make one from recycled materials, such as coffee cans and lids, oatmeal boxes, and paint stirrers.

"Five Little Apples" Finger Play

What? Use simple, accessible, and inexpensive materials to make finger puppets to use when singing songs and doing finger plays like "Five Little Apples."

Why? Puppets are an effective way to help children pay attention and get involved while singing a song or doing a finger play. The puppets stimulate the visual and kinesthetic senses that support listening. Children can participate in finger plays by imitating simple movements and the rhythm and rhyme of a repeated vocal refrain.

How? Purchase a package of inexpensive cotton work gloves at a hardware store or online. They are sold by the dozen.

- Wash and dry the gloves so the fabric shrinks (this makes them thicker so they last longer).
- Choose decorative items included in a song or finger game (for example, small wooden fruits, rubber animals, or flowers).
- Glue or Velcro one item on each finger. Make a glove for yourself and one for each child.

Wear a glove puppet when singing a song or doing a finger play. To introduce this finger play, wear a cotton glove with a wooden apple on each finger.

Extensions. Play a slide whistle to give auditory cues while pretending to climb up and down the tree.

After repeating the song and fingerplay a few times, invite children to take turns wearing the gloves and playing the slide whistle.

REFERENCE

Schafer, R.M. 1993. *The Soundscape: Our Sonic Environment and the Tuning of the World.* Rochester, VT: Destiny Books.

Music and Movement Learning Center Checklist

Laura J. Colker

You can complete this checklist for the music and movement learning center in your classroom on your own or with a teaching colleague. When you are finished, review the items you rated as "rarely" and create an action plan to help change the rating to "sometimes" or "regularly."

	Regularly	Sometimes	Rarely
1. Children choose to play in the music and movement center every day.	○	○	○
2. Children know and follow the rules for using the music and movement center.	○	○	○
3. The center is located away from quieter areas, such as the language and literacy center.	○	○	○
4. Materials are stored in labeled containers and shelves within children's reach.	○	○	○
5. There are books about musicians and music.	○	○	○
6. There is enough space for children to move freely, without bumping into objects or each other.	○	○	○
7. Children have fun and express pleasure in making and moving to music.	○	○	○
8. While playing in the music and movement center, children express thoughts and feelings and build skills in all domains.	○	○	○
9. The music and movement center has			
• Recorded music of various cultures and genres and headphones for individual use	○	○	○
• Photos and illustrations of instruments, musicians, and dancers representing diverse cultures	○	○	○
• Various rhythm instruments—two or more of each kind	○	○	○
• Items that children use to sing, and to create and learn about music and dance	○	○	○
10. Teachers extend children's play by			
• Engaging children in conversations	○	○	○
• Asking questions	○	○	○
• Responding to children's questions	○	○	○
• Offering ideas	○	○	○
• Commenting on children's explorations and creations	○	○	○
• Providing new props that offer different experiences and challenges	○	○	○

Dramatic Play

Oral Storytelling: Building Community Through Dialogue, Engagement, and Problem Solving

Doriet Berkowitz

Ariel says, "Tell me a story." As I begin, more children gather to listen. They offer suggestions as their eyes widen. Together, we act out familiar stories.

We frequently read stories from illustrated books, but my coteacher Veda and I tell oral stories too. Oral storytelling supports children's learning and development differently than stories read aloud from books. It allows children to use their imagination, communicate effectively, increase their social awareness, and build community. Many skills practiced through oral storytelling and dramatic play also support early learning standards.

Building Community

With each new group of 3-year-olds, I start the school year by telling stories. In our classroom we gather as an entire community twice a day.

The children and I make eye contact without a book between us. As we read each other's faces and emotions, a call-and-response takes place. If I suddenly jump up or raise my voice, the children gasp. If I whisper, they crouch forward. Our listening and response communication creates a level of intimacy and unity at these gatherings.

Listening, Participating, Learning

One morning, I tell the story of "Goldilocks and the Three Bears." I stop at appropriate times so the children can act out the story. I invite them to hold the tiny bowl of porridge that Goldilocks finishes. They cup their palms to make the bowl and taste the porridge. They rock back and forth, pretending to sit on a rocking chair. At the end of the story, Goldilocks wakes up frightened and runs away. The children spontaneously stomp their feet in place to mimic Goldilocks fleeing.

Teachers can find moments in stories to intensify through performance. Tell a familiar story and choose these moments spontaneously. Plan in advance with newer stories. Performing a story brings the words to life and grabs children's attention.

By acting out stories, children note how characters look, move, and sound. They consider each character's unique traits and develop gestures and words to make them real. Ask children questions like "How does this troll move his arms when he speaks?" or "How does the eldest Billy Goat Gruff sound different from the Baby Goat?" This questioning helps them distinguish characters' various sizes and attitudes. In addition, it helps children develop awareness and sensitivity to different points of view.

By engaging in purposeful storytelling actions, children's physical experiences can help them remember the story better and connect with it more personally. For example, as I told "Goldilocks and the Three Bears," the children felt the weight and temperature of the bowl of porridge; they felt the jolting contrast between peaceful sleep and sudden flight; they used a natural sense of timing and volume to switch from stillness to suddenly stomping their feet. Young children develop a deeper concept of space, time, movement, sound, and rhythm when they physically participate in telling a story.

Getting to Know a Story

Telling children a familiar story or inviting them to join in with a repetitive phrase in a story helps them feel comfortable and confident. Children anticipate the pattern and join in. For example, "We're Going on a Lion Hunt," Aubrey Davis's *The Enormous Potato*, and Linda Williams's *The Little Old Lady Who Was Not Afraid of Anything* engage preschoolers and invite them to recognize patterns and remember repetitive phrases. In "The Three Billy Goats Gruff," the repeated *trip-trap-trip-trap* as the goats cross the bridge provides predictability and familiarity.

Months ago, my coteacher Veda invented a story about four characters named the Pinky Sisters. She tells it in installments, offering a new story each day. The same group of five children requests a Pinky Sisters story. They make suggestions, and Veda incorporates their ideas so they directly impact the story. For example, Veda named the characters the "Pinky Sisters" because two girls in the group regularly wear pink. As Veda told the story of how the sisters met a monster one day, the children interrupted. They said the monster should be big, green, and become their friend. Thus, the plot and characters in the Pinky Sisters stories keeps growing.

Engaging Children in Drama

Oral storytelling naturally leads to dramatic presentations. Children gain a sense of confidence and control as they imagine and act out characters and events. They often find solutions to challenges.

One morning, 3-year-old Anna watches a baby praying mantis creeping along the playground fence. When we return indoors, she pulls out a plastic praying mantis from our toy insect collection. "My praying mantis is sick," she says. "He got smushed in your pocket. I need to fix him." Then she takes apart a toy stethoscope and connects the tubes to the front legs of the plastic praying mantis. "There you go," she tells it, "you are all better now."

Oral storytelling helps Anna imagine the insect's changing condition. In her pretend play, Anna has the power to improve the insect's condition. By reasoning aloud she discovers what is wrong, what must be done, and whether the solution works. She is glad when the insect recovers, and feels responsible for its positive change. Oral storytelling allows Anna to make sense of the praying mantis's struggle. Later she may apply this understanding to herself when she is sick.

Problem Solving

When preschoolers make predictions, put a sequence of events together, or interpret tone and mood, they develop the skills necessary for learning to read and to interact well with others. As young children take turns communicating with each other, they see different points of view and work together to solve problems. They develop the language and understanding to negotiate plans and solutions and become aware of the consequences of their actions.

The following conversation shows Ramon's emerging understanding that he can change and make different decisions.

• •

Ramon [frowning]: When I grow up, I'm going to be a giant. I'm going to eat people up.

Ariel: I'm going to be a happy giant.

Ramon: I'm going to be a grumpy giant. [Pause] But a giant needs friends.

Ramon continues thinking about the topic the next day.

Ramon: When I grow up, I'm going to be a giant that eats everyone up.

Teacher: Will you eat your friends up?

Ramon: Yes.

Teacher: Who will you play with if you eat your friends and they won't be with you anymore?

Ramon: They'll be with me in my belly. [Pause] The second time I grow up, I'll be a giant and I won't eat my friends.

Over time, Ramon reflects on what he imagined was true before and shapes a new model for what he thinks is true now.

Though illustrations are important in supporting children's literacy development, sometimes pictures can limit a child's imagining. Oral storytelling challenges children to create their own visuals. When children take information they hear and transform it into their own images and meanings, they use the same inventiveness necessary for problem solving.

Conclusion

Oral storytelling encourages deeper participation among preschoolers through role-playing and performance. Preschoolers develop important speaking and listening skills when they express their ideas and respond to those of others.

Storytelling can support young children's creativity and cognitive, language, social, and emotional development. Teachers can also record (by writing or using audio or videotape) the children's conversations and document their interactions. Documenting this development over time allows teachers and families to mark milestones in children's thinking and understanding of life experiences. Often documentation uncovers themes in children's observations and questions that teachers can incorporate in the curriculum.

Supporting Dual Language Learners

Oral storytelling is a rich tradition that is seen in many cultures. Most preschool classrooms have one or more children who speak different languages. Thus, storytelling plans should include strategies that make all children feel included. Invite family members, assistants, and volunteers who can communicate with children who are dual language learners to be part of the storytelling activity. Provide extra support for volunteers by sharing the tips in this article. When telling a story in a language that is new to some of the children, learn and use a few key words in their home languages. This can help everyone make the connections they need to truly enjoy this rich learning experience.

Tips for Oral Storytelling

- Learn a few simple stories. Use fairy tales, folktales, and stories from your life.
- Tell stories with phrases that repeat and can be easily remembered and predicted by children. "Goldilocks and the Three Bears," "We're Going on a Lion Hunt," Aubrey Davis's *The Enormous Potato*, and Linda Williams's *The Little Old Lady Who Was Not Afraid of Anything* are examples of these kinds of stories.
- Identify parts in the story when children can perform physically or express themselves through words and sounds. Invite children to act out or make sounds for these parts.

- Ask questions related to the story that prompt children's imagination and support comprehension. For example, "Why do you think Goldilocks chose to sleep in the baby bear's bed?" or "How do you think she feels once she finds the perfect chair?"
- Retell stories that children enjoy. The more familiar they become with a story or character, the more they will want to perform it independently.
- Understand and accept that children may interrupt. This means they are engaged and wish to share their ideas. Find ways to integrate their ideas in the story without losing momentum.

Dramatic Play Learning Center

Amy Laura Dombro

What Children Do and Learn

Language and Literacy

- Talk about what they are doing during their pretend play scenarios.
- Join in conversations with teachers and classmates.

Math

- Count how many seats are in the rocket ship. "One, two, three."
- Use one-to-one correspondence to line up three chairs for the three patients waiting to see the doctor.
- Recognize numbers while making and reading a grocery list: 7 bananas, 4 pears, 5 mangos . . .

Deepen Understanding of Self and Others

- Gain a sense of control by taking on the roles of adults such as firefighters and doctors.
- Incorporate community helpers in their dramatic play by pretending to be a teacher, restaurant cook, or construction worker.

Social and Emotional

- Make and carry out a plan together.
- Take turns playing different roles and using different props and costumes.
- Negotiate and compromise about plans and use of materials.

Beyond the Basics

- Incorporate other classroom activities into children's dramatic play. Did you bake bread together? Add photos from the project, a bread pan, and a copy of the recipe to the children's kitchen area.
- Extend children's play by asking questions or offering ideas: "What do you see out the window as you ride the train? Here are markers and paper in case you want to draw what you see."
- Read books with children that reflect their current dramatic play interests or inspire new ones.

Include Children's Families and Cultures

- Invite family members to contribute items from their home cultures—empty food boxes, children's books, photos, props, clothes and music CDs—to ensure that every child feels at home in the dramatic play area.
- Post (on a bulletin board or online) photos and brief written observations of children's dramatic play to share with families. Invite families to share their photos of and observations about children's play at home.
- Invite family members to come in and talk with children about their work and interests. A bus driver, a doorman, a scientist, or a nurse can inspire new play themes, as can a parent who gardens or bakes.

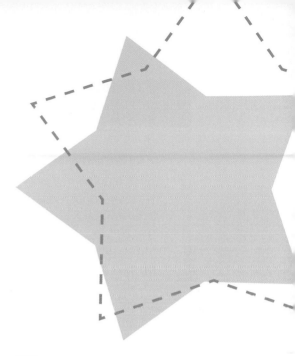

A Place for Puppets

Laura J. Colker

A place for puppets, housed in the dramatic play center, offers children opportunities to make puppets, write scripts, and perform puppet shows. Children can work through their feelings and re-create the plots of books. As they play with puppets, children can develop language and literacy, math, and art skills.

Materials—Puppetry requires puppets or a variety of materials for making puppets. Children need storybooks and paper, markers, and other materials for writing scripts and making tickets. With a puppet stage, children can perform for an audience.

Puppets

Teachers and children can make puppets to play the characters in a story or represent animals, family members, or community helpers. See "Ways to Make Puppets" on page 88.

Purchased puppets are likely to inspire many different kinds of puppet shows.

- Finger puppets are fun for putting on a miniature show in a shoe box.
- Molded plastic and rubber hand puppets are easy to wash and tend to be long lasting.
- Furry animal puppets are realistic and cozy in the same way as stuffed animals.
- Oversized puppets can sit on a teacher's lap and engage the children in conversation.
- Big-mouthed puppets inspire talkative characters who engage with each other and the audience.
- Family puppets come in diverse sets to mix and match depending on children's cultures and the composition of their families.

What Children Do and Learn

Language and Literacy
- Act out a story after hearing it read.
- Write a script for a puppet show.
- Place letters on a flannel board.

Math
- Glue googly eyes on a sock puppet face.
- Cut fabric to make curtains for the puppet stage.
- Hand out one ticket to each audience member.

Art
- Make a puppet version of a favorite book character, such as *The Very Hungry Caterpillar*.
- Put on a puppet skit of a visit to the dentist.

Setup Tips

- Place open shelving next to the table so children can easily reach supplies.
- Provide books about puppets and storybooks to inspire play writing.
- Use baskets to store props.
- Keep the puppet theater area clear so children can get into and out of it easily.
- Post photos or posters of puppets from various cultures on the wall. Underneath each puppet, note which children share that tradition.

Budget Stretchers

- Look for puppet props such as doll-sized hats, purses, scarves, crowns, and wands at thrift shops, dollar stores, and yard sales.
- Ask families to donate brown paper lunch bags, old (washed) socks, balloons, fabric scraps, and other puppet-making supplies.

Include Children's Families and Cultures

- Invite families to attend puppet show performances.
- Ask families to suggest books, folk tales, songs, and story ideas that children can turn into plays.
- Hold a family workshop to make an inexpensive puppet theater. This website offers ideas of varying complexity: http://bluepurpleandscarlett.com/2011/08/26/a-home-made-puppet-theater

Ways to Make Puppets

Meghan Dombrink-Green

Puppets help bring children's play to life. Creating scenarios for different characters can increase children's vocabularies and storytelling skills and provide a safe way to express challenging feelings. And putting on a puppet show is just plain fun! Make some of these puppets with the preschoolers in your class.

Two-Stick or Dragon Puppet

Supplies: *colored paper, scissors, markers or crayons, glue, tape, Popsicle sticks or cardboard, extras*

- Draw the head and tail of the dragon on colored paper.
- Cut out the head and tail.
- Cut another piece of colored paper in half lengthwise.
- Fold the two pieces, using accordion folds. Tape them together to make one long piece.
- Glue or tape one end of the folded paper to the dragon head and one end to the dragon tail.
- Glue or tape a Popsicle stick to the dragon head and another one to the dragon tail.
- Decorate with extras to make the puppet more colorful.

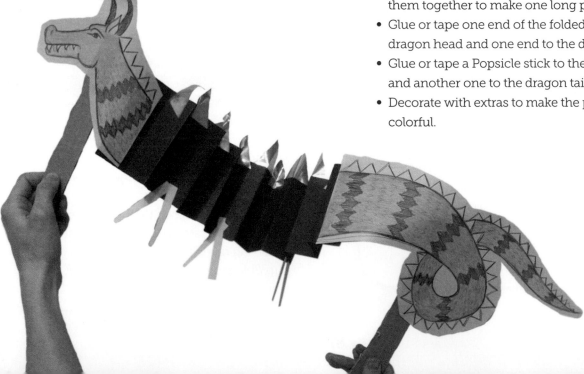

Felt Puppet

Supplies: *felt in multiple colors (at least two pieces), scissors, markers, glue, extras*

- Trace the desired puppet shape on two pieces of felt and cut them out.
- Put the shapes together and glue at the edges. Leave an opening for the hand.
- Decorate with felt scraps and use extras to add hair, clothes, eyes, and other features.

Finger Puppet

Supplies: *old glove, scissors, glue, markers, extras*

- Cut the fingers off the glove where they meet the hand. Put the hand part in the scrap box.
- Decorate each finger with markers or extras.

Jointed Puppet

Supplies: *cardboard, glue, scissors, markers or crayons, metal paper fasteners, Popsicle sticks, extras*

- Cut out the desired puppet shape from the cardboard. Decorate it.
- Cut off the arms and legs.
- Poke holes in the body, near where the arms and legs were joined to it. Poke holes in the arms and legs, near the cut ends.
- Reattach the arms and legs, lining up the holes and securing the limbs with metal paper fasteners.
- Glue the finished puppet onto a Popsicle stick or piece of cardboard.

Shadow Puppet

Supplies: *poster board, scissors, tape, straws or Popsicle sticks, a large piece of cardboard, white paper, a table lamp or flashlight*

- Cut the desired shape for your puppet out of the poster board.
- Tape the puppet to a straw or Popsicle stick.
- To make a freestanding screen, fold back the ends of the cardboard so it stands on its own.
- Cut out a large rectangular space from the middle of the cardboard. This will be the screen for the puppets.
- Tape white paper over the cut-out space.
- Shine the table lamp or flashlight behind the screen and grab your puppet. Hold the puppet between the light and the screen. The audience in front will see the puppet shadow.

Unstuffed Animal Puppet

Supplies: *preloved stuffed animal, glue or sewing needle and thread*

- Purchase stuffed animals from garage sales or thrift stores.
- Determine where the puppeteer's hand will go, and cut an opening there in the animal.
- Remove most of the stuffing, but leave the head filled.
- Finish the edges of the hand hole with hand-sewn stitching or glue.

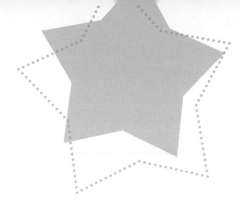

Paper Bag Puppet

Supplies: *paper bag, pencil/pen/marker, glue, extras*

- Lay a paper bag flat, with the bottom folded face up at the top. The bottom flap will be the face.
- Add eyes, a nose, and a mouth.
- Stick your hand in the paper bag and use your fingers and thumb to move the puppet's mouth.

Sock Puppet

Supplies: *sock, marker, scissors, cardboard, fabric, glue, extras*

- Put your hand in the sock, with fingers in the toe area and wrist in the heel.
- Form a mouth in the sock using your thumb and fingers. With a marker, draw a straight line where the mouth is.
- Remove the sock from your hand and cut along the line.
- Cut out two ovals, three inches wide and five inches long, one from the cardboard and one from the fabric.
- Glue the fabric oval onto the cardboard oval.
- Fold the oval in half, fabric side in.
- Glue the oval in the mouth hole of the sock.
- Decorate the sock puppet.

Extras for Personalizing Puppets

- Pom-poms, many colors
- Feathers
- Yarn
- Googly eyes
- Pipe cleaners
- Ribbon
- Paper strips/curls
- Fabric scraps

Pretend Play Leads to Real-Life Learning

Laura J. Colker

Social and Emotional

What do children learn by dressing up and role-playing as firefighters, doctors, or construction workers?

What social skills does it take to work together during dramatic play (for example, as firefighters)?

How could pretending to examine a patient help a child overcome her fear of doctors?

Learning through role playing: By imitating a firefighter using a hose, a doctor checking a patient's ear, or a construction worker building a skyscraper, children learn about community roles and services and feel proud and satisfied. While acting as mothers and fathers, children can be caring, loving, and responsible.

Grocery store staff, construction workers, restaurant staff, and farmers feel useful, needed, and accomplished.

Coping with fears: Pretend play allows children to explore their fears in a safe setting. A child can begin to conquer her fear of doctors by donning a lab coat and stethoscope and becoming the person who scares her. She replaces her fear with a sense of control.

Working together: Firefighters need to negotiate: Who will drive the fire truck? Who will rescue the baby? Whether fighting fires, serving and cleaning up after a meal, or feeding the cows, children must plan, compromise, cooperate, share, and communicate.

Cognitive

What might a child learn about math and science while bagging pretend groceries?

What can a grocery store scenario teach children about money?

What problem-solving skills might children work on?

What other thinking skills do children use during pretend play?

Math and science: As he fills a bag with groceries, a child learns that objects take up space and that the bag will hold only those items that will fit in the space inside it. Shoppers give the clerk money and the clerk gives them change. This exercise acquaints children with bills and coins, and they begin to understand the purpose of money. They also explore concepts related to adding and subtracting.

Problem-solving skills: The girls with the cows (see p. 95) might decide how much grass to feed them. Below, the boy washing dishes might find a way to separate the clean utensils from the dirty ones.

Thinking skills: When they pretend, children create pictures in their minds of past experiences and use their imaginations to think of new scenarios. These thoughts and images let children think about situations and objects that are not right in front of them and events that have not yet happened.

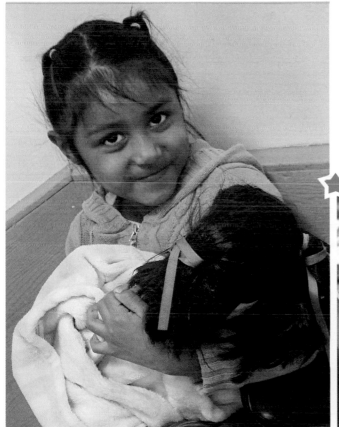

Language and Literacy

What vocabulary could a teacher introduce to preschoolers?

How can pretend play encourage their language development?

How could a teacher incorporate early writing skills into dramatic play?

Vocabulary: Lots of rich vocabulary words are associated with the play pictured here: stethoscope, suds, hard hat, grocery scanner, cash register, cud, menu, sign-in sheet, and clipboard, for example.

Language development: When using a phone, a child must speak aloud, anticipate what an imaginary speaker on the other end of the line would say, and reply accordingly. Pretend play encourages conversations about topics such as:

- What are all the groceries for—a picnic, dinner, visiting company?
- How long is the wait at the doctor's office? At the restaurant?
- Why did you call?
- Where are you and your baby going on the bus?

Early writing skills: A clipboard and pen on a desk invite children to sign in at the doctor's, dentist's, or vet's office. Likewise, the sign in the restaurant lets diners know they need to wait to be seated. By helping children post the sign and by sitting in the restaurant, the teacher encourages reading and writing.

Physical

How do children build small motor skills through pretend play?

How does pretend play strengthen hand-eye coordination?

Small motor development: Washing dishes, putting on fancy shoes, using a medical tool to examine a patient's ear, dialing a phone, hammering, writing, and bagging groceries—all are ways children can build small motor skills during pretend play.

Hand-eye coordination: When using props, children have to coordinate their eye and hand movements. Grocery clerks have to place items in bags, construction workers use hammers, and everyone has to put their shoes on the correct feet.

Extending the Learning

What could a teacher say or do to build on children's learning during pretend play?

How might a teacher document progress related to learning standards?

Build on children's learning during play:
- Pick up another phone and talk with the child on the phone.
- Place a rubber pig on the table with the cows and say, "This pig doesn't like grass. What can you feed him?"
- Ask two girls who are dressing up, "Where are you going?"

A teacher could also pose some thinking questions:
- What would you do if you ran out of water or if the fire truck broke down?
- How can you make sure the building won't topple over?
- What will you do while waiting for your turn?

Document learning related to standards: After formally observing children and taking photos similar to the ones shown here, a teacher could match this evidence of learning to state or program standards. A series of photographs and notes could show individual children cooperating, writing, using fine motor skills, solving problems, talking, and thinking creatively.

Books That Tell Folktales

Lauren Baker

Folktales are oral histories passed down from generation to generation. They offer cultural awareness, legend, and imaginative narratives that preschoolers can act out using props or by making puppets and creating a puppet show.

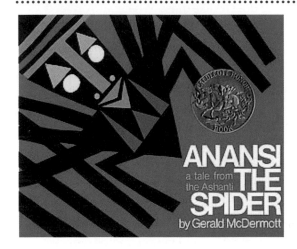

Anansi the Spider: A Tale from the Ashanti, by Gerald McDermott. 1972. Henry Holt and Company.

Anansi the Spider is the West African Ashanti's favorite trickster. When Anansi is in trouble, his children draw on their skills, come together as a team, and save the day. This book is a fabulous example of children maintaining individuality while working together as a team.

Thunder Cake, by Patricia Polacco. 1990. Philomel Books.

CRACK! Lightning sears the sky and a little girl runs to her grandmother. This touching folktale explains the legend behind loud storms through the story of a child and her grandmother. The recipe for Thunder Cake appears on the last page of the book.

Moon Rope/Un lazo a la luna, by Lois Ehlert. 1992. Harcourt.

This folktale explains the origin of the "man in the moon." The story begins when Fox and Mole decide to take a trip to the moon. It isn't long before the characters learn that getting to the moon is not nearly as hard as getting back to Earth. Preschoolers will identify with the characters' vivid personalities.

Joseph Had a Little Overcoat, by Simms Taback. 1999. Viking Children's Books.

This story teaches readers that it is always possible to make something out of nothing. The die-cut in the illustrations are creative and show the changes to Joseph's coat. The story's sequencing makes it easy and fun for preschoolers to predict what words come next.

After Reading These Books

Tell the stories. Draw on storytelling traditions to tell these folktales. Use props, like clothing from the cultures in the stories. Create story boxes filled with materials related to the stories. These boxes can include costumes, puppets, props, and hats that you and the children can use to retell the stories.

Celebrate cultural diversity. Preschoolers, as experts of their own community, can explore the places where other people live. Learn about the different countries these stories come from by listening to their music or sampling traditional foods. On a world map, mark the country and your location with stickers. Put the map in the classroom where children can see and discuss it.

Invite children to tell their stories. Encourage children to share experiences from their lives or something make-believe. Put a voice-recording device in the dramatic play area so children can record the stories and then play them back for themselves and their friends. They can also work in small groups to act out their stories for the class.

Creating and Using Prop Boxes

Derry Koralek

Why do this activity? A prop box is a collection of items, stored in an easy to carry container with a lid, all of which are related to a specific theme or activity of interest to preschoolers. Prop boxes are a way to build on or expand children's interests, offer new challenges, and introduce new activities.

What can children learn? Learning depends on the content and theme of the prop pox. For example, if the prop box focuses on pretend play, such as an auto re-pair shop, preschoolers can solve problems, learn social skills, and be creative. If the prop box includes items for making puzzles, children are likely to build small motor, creative, and thinking skills.

Vocabulary words: *prop, any words being explored as a part of the prop box theme*

Materials:
- Clear plastic storage bins, cardboard file boxes, or paper boxes from a copy shop (to serve as the prop box)
- Labels and markers
- Theme-related props and materials

Prepare for the Activity

1. Consider children's current skills and interests, then involve them in choosing a few prop box themes such as pet shop, camping, or puzzle making. Teachers and children may choose to create prop boxes that go with a curriculum theme or that are related to a shared experience such as a field trip.
2. Collect and acquire relevant materials to use in prop boxes. Items can be gathered or donated by teachers, families, and community members.
3. Set up a place to work. Arrange prop box materials on a table for children to inspect.

Lead Small Groups

1. Invite four to six children to participate.
2. Discuss the materials on the table and how they might be used. Give children time to explore them. Notice how children engage with the materials and use their imaginations to assign meaning to the objects.
3. Work with the children to organize and label the prop boxes by theme.
4. Place prop boxes in the appropriate learning center or other easily accessible place.

Respond to Individual Needs

Make boxes to address individual interests and skills. For example, every day before Kamilah comes to school, she watches the crew painting her family's house, and Yancey caught a fish and cooked it when he went on a picnic with his grandparents. Their teacher uses this information to create prop boxes.

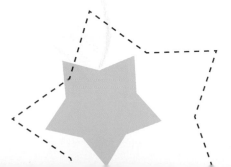

Follow Up After the Activity

Create new prop boxes or add or exchange items in the current boxes. Put away a box when children are not longer using it. Some children might make the boxes their own, adding and replacing objects as their interests change.

Involve Families

1. Ask families to donate materials for classroom prop boxes. Outgrown clothes, old toys, or spare keys can all make interesting props for children to explore.
2. Write a handout or web article to explain how children use prop boxes in the classroom. Or, introduce the contents of a prop box at a family meeting. Suggest that families make prop boxes for children to use at home.

Engineering With
The Three Little Pigs

Maureen Ingram

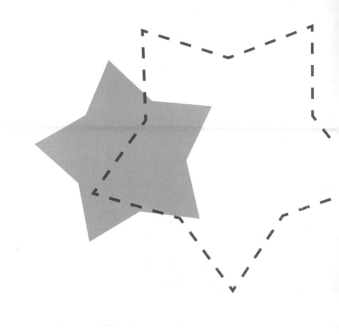

Why do this activity? The story of the three little pigs provides an introduction to the design process integral to engineering. Preschoolers instinctively see the game in the engineering process—building something and testing to see if it works.

What can children learn? Children identify a problem, design and construct a solution, and then test the accuracy of their solution. It is natural for preschoolers to be engineers because of their love of hands-on construction, their ability to use materials in new ways, and their limitless curiosity about the world.

Vocabulary words: *engineering, test, design, problem, solution, prediction, structure, recyclables*

Materials:
- *The Three Little Pigs* storybook
- Pencils
- Paper
- Masking tape
- Cardboard
- Blow-dryer
- Recycled materials such as empty cereal boxes, milk jugs, egg cartons, and plastic containers

Prepare for the Activity

1. Read the story of *The Three Little Pigs* to the children. Discuss the characters and the plot. Then review the text by asking recall questions such as *How many pigs are there? What is the first house built of? And the second house? The third house?* The answers will help children during the engineering activity.
2. Arrange materials on a table for children to use and explore in groups of four.

Lead Small Groups

1. Define the problem. In the folktale, the Big Bad Wolf is trying to blow the pigs' houses down. Challenge the children: *Can you build a house that the wolf cannot blow down?*
2. Create a plan. Provide pencils and paper for the children to create an engineering drawing. Remind them to include all the details for what makes their house structure strong. (For very young children who are eager to get building, consider revisiting this step after the house has been built. At that point they can create an observational drawing of the final structure.)
3. Build the structure. Provide masking tape and scissors and have children select two or three recyclables with which to begin building. They can use tape to connect the pieces. (For ongoing engineering explorations, ask families to donate recyclables. In general, cardboard is easiest for preschoolers to fasten, rather than plastic, glass, or other materials.)
4. Test the structure. This engineering activity needs a wolf, and a blow-dryer is just the thing! For younger preschoolers, the teacher can be the wolf. Older children can take turns. After each child has constructed a house, set up a test site in the classroom. Encourage teamwork by having children observe each other's tests and cheer each other on.

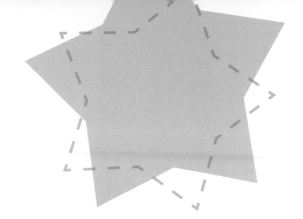

Make sure to prepare children for failure. It is likely that someone's house will fall over during testing. Remind them that engineers love when this happens. Challenges and setbacks are opportunities to get thinking: *Why didn't that work? How might we modify the house so it is stronger?* If the structure fails, then begin again with Step 1.

Respond to Individual Needs

Ask children open-ended questions to encourage thinking.

- What keeps a house from blowing over?
- Tell me about what you have built. What is the purpose of this part of your structure?
- How might you make your structure stronger?
- What is your prediction—will the wolf blow it over or will it stay strong?
- What are the similarities and differences between these houses?

Follow Up After the Activity

Share the results. After each test, help children reflect on what happened, what worked, and what would change the results. Take photos of the structures and tests so children can revisit their work.

Involve Families

Challenge families to complete a similar project at home. Have them take pictures of the completed structure to share with the class. Invite children—and their families, if they would like to join—to share the photos and results of this experiment with their classmates.

Resources

Building a House, by Byron Barton
Three Little Pigs, by Paul Galdone
How a House Is Built, by Gail Gibbons
Look at That Building: A First Book of Structures, by Scot Ritchie
If I Built a House, by Chris Van Dusen

The author was inspired by the Children's Engineering workshop, taught by Vince Walencik and Liz Kendall of Montclair State University, New Jersey.

Using Improvisational Play to Support Social Skills

Barbara E. O'Neill

In September, 4-year-old John played alone in the block corner each day. He made small stacks of blocks, banged blocks together, and knocked over other children's structures. He spoke using just one or two words.

Now, at the end of the school year, John plays by himself in the housekeeping area. He puts a baby doll on the table and covers her with a blanket. John asks me, "Want to be the mom?" I tell him I cannot play just now.

John approaches one child and then another. He travels from table to table, asking children, "Want to be the mom?" By the time he asks the seventh child, I am concerned—will anyone say yes? Just then Leilani smiles enthusiastically, takes Javan's hand, says "Come on," and they follow John back to the housekeeping area.

The three children play house for half an hour. Leilani is the mother, Javan is the sister, and John is the dog. During their cooperative play, John announces his role ("I'm the dog"), transforms objects ("Here are my dog biscuits"), builds on Leilani's and Javan's ideas, and uses what is for him elaborate language ("Leilani, you and I go to the grocery store, buy chocolate ice cream?").

In most preschool classrooms there are some children who struggle during playtime. When they also have developmental delays, such children may have difficulty playing, talking, and learning with their peers. Leading activities based on theater improvisation—improv—is one way to creatively and playfully help preschoolers develop social skills. Like open-ended dramatic play, improv activities can respond to children's interests and encourage them to develop new skills.

To begin a three-person play group, I say to the children, "Your job is to get better at playing *together.*" I tell them that we need to create, in improv terms, "an ensemble." Our improv ensemble will work together to create a scene by accepting and building on one another's offers—the things they say and do. All players are active creators of the play. Thus all have a role in developing the performance.

"Yes, and": The Basics of Improv

This simple storytelling activity helps children learn how to accept and build on each other's offers—the basis of all improv activity. The children work together to create a story with each sentence beginning with the words "Yes, and."

I begin the game by having the children sit with me in a circle. Then I ask them what they would like to call the story. I typically accept the first answer a child calls out. Once the story has a title, I start the game by offering the first sentence, such as "Yesterday, Sasha and her mother went to the park." Next, children take turns adding on to this story, beginning each sentence with the phrase "yes, and." For example, a child might choose to add to my offer (the sentence above) by saying "Yes, and Sasha went on the slide," or "Yes, and Sasha fell and hurt her knee." Children can pass a ball or other small object around the circle so it is clear whose turn it is to talk.

At first children might be hesitant to join in and not know what to say. Sometimes a gentle prompt helps

Supporting Dual Language Learners

It can be wonderful when children who speak different languages find ways to come together for sophisticated play as an "ensemble." They may need extra support to overcome language barriers to successfully participate in this activity. Sometimes, children with different languages or abilities end up being followers because it is hard for their plans and ideas to be heard. One of the most important things for teachers and peers to do is listen patiently so that dual language learners can feel comfortable as they share their ideas or direct the play scenario. Also, teach children to pick up nonverbal communication cues. It is important to model this patient, attentive listening so that all of the children have a valued role in play. We want children to understand that classmates who speak different languages don't always communicate verbally, but their brains are just as full of ideas. If we learn to listen carefully, we can learn about their ideas.

them respond. If this does not help, move on, but be sure to offer each child a turn every time the object comes around. As they practice collective storytelling, children often forget about getting it "right" and get caught up in the story. The focus becomes the story-telling—not individual performance.

Nonverbal Improv Games

Children who seldom or never talk are at a significant disadvantage in the play group. Mirror, Mirror is an improv game that doesn't require speaking. There are two rules to the game—copy one another and use only nonsense words or gibberish. The game can be played in pairs, or a trio can play with all three group members copying one another.

When I first play this game with children, I quickly explain the game's rules and then prompt them to copy me, explaining that I will soon copy them. I might make a face, jump, or make a silly noise. They copy me, but also sometimes look at one another or engage in off-task behavior such as laughing, making silly faces, or picking up a nearby toy. I consider these behaviors to be offers and copy them. Sometimes when the children do something by accident, I copy that. Teachers can take children's silly initiations as offers and use them to move the game along. Mirror, Mirror lets children respond to one another socially without relying on language.

Improv During Dramatic Play

Teachers can also use improv principles in the dramatic play center during choice time. During improv play groups a teacher leads the activities, but in choice

time the children take the lead. Teachers can join in and look for offers so they can extend the play. At the same time, they make sure the children are in control of the way the play transforms.

In applying improv principles to dramatic play, teachers need to accept and build on the children's choices, while offering encouragement based on children's needs. Children do not have to be anything other than what they choose to be, even if they choose to be the same thing every time. No one is assigned a certain role or behavior, just as an improv performer has no script. Instead, as we learn to work together creatively in a positive and accepting environment, players can take a risk and try a new role in response to another player's offer.

For example, in dramatic play, John always played the role of a dog. While I was concerned about him taking only one role, when we used improv I always accepted this as his offer. I trusted he would be inspired to take on other roles over time. In addition to giving

him ample time to be the dog in whatever way he wanted, I frequently made my own offers to encourage him to act this role in new ways. I offered him pretend dog biscuits and suggested other things a dog might do.

Conclusion

During the last week of school, I asked the children, "What are we learning in the play group?" John quickly replied, "Play blocks, play food, play big trucks." John had indeed developed his capacity to play blocks with Keol, to play with food in the house area with Leilani, and to play with big trucks with Javan. Javan added, "Yeah! And we play together." He drew out the word together, mimicking the way I often emphasized it. "Yes," I said, "Remember when playing together was really hard for us?" Javan nodded. "I was just thinking that. Now we play together," he said with a smile. John smiled too and said, "Play together! Can we play with trains?" Javan and I immediately took John up on his offer by setting out the trains. "And let's pretend there are dogs on the train and they are getting all dressed up!" added Javan. And we did.

Improv Play Intervention—Tips for Teachers

- Set aside time each day to have a play group with designated children during choice time or center time.
- Establish and play with consistent small groups that include children with different strengths and needs. Include only one child who struggles during playtime.
- Provide open-ended materials in the dramatic play center that children can use in unconventional ways.
- Develop key phrases and use child-friendly language that conveys that the play group is a time to get better at playing together.
- Ask questions about how the group is working together to help the children see themselves as creators of the group's activity and process.
- Look for unexpected offers and consider playful ways to build on them.

Reflective Questions

Children's desire to play together often brings with it the challenge of communicating and negotiating differing perspectives and ideas. As you reflect on the ideas from this article, consider these questions.

Know Yourself
Think about your own life. How comfortable are you in a scripted world where there is a schedule and rules to follow? Where and when do you step out of the script? Does it feel risky? Are you penalized for breaking out of the norm? Rewarded? How does this impact your work with children?

Consider the Children's Perspectives
The author describes how she accepts children's offers even when she has a different idea about what she would like to happen. As you try this approach, notice which offers you accept easily and which you accept with difficulty. Try taking the child's point of view as you think about what he is trying to accomplish. How does this impact your willingness to go with his ideas? What do you notice about children's responses when you say yes to their offers?

Examine the Environment
The author recommends offering open-ended props and materials to encourage more possibilities for children's dramatic play roles. Observe children using the materials in your environment. What ideas and inventions do you see and hear the children exploring? Which materials enhance and extend their play? How do the materials help the children build on each other's ideas?

What's in Your Dramatic Play Center?

compiled by Lauren Baker

Preschoolers engage in a variety of creative activities in the dramatic play center. When teachers introduce new props and materials, children can incorporate them in more sophisticated play. Here are some interesting, open-ended items to expand children's imaginations.

- Loose parts, such as yarn, pinecones, seeds, acorns, and recyclables such as bottle caps
- Cardboard boxes
- Masking tape, duct tape, and colorful paper tape
- Measuring tapes, yardsticks, rulers, and other tools

- Flashlights, candles, and lamps
- Pool noodles (cut in different lengths)
- Cardboard tubes from rolls of paper towels or wrapping paper
- Baskets, buckets, laundry baskets, and other large and small containers
- Clean, empty food and product boxes, plastic bottles, and containers
- Carpet squares or tile samples
- Donations from local businesses, such as menus, flowers, and take-out containers
- Small sheets, fabric pieces, scarves, or blankets for making costumes and structures
- Real items, such as phones, keyboards, microfiber dusters with handles, non-toxic plants, placemats, unbreakable mirrors
- Newspapers, magazines, tickets, and order pads
- Paper, markers, crayons, and pencils
- Children's books that reflect the children's interests, families, and cultures

Listen carefully to children and engage them in conversations. Include items in the center that reflect their interests.

Dramatic Play Learning Center Checklist

Laura J. Colker

 You can complete this checklist for the dramatic play center in your classroom on your own, or with a teaching colleague. When you are finished, review the items you rated as "rarely" and create an action plan to help change the rating to "sometimes" or "regularly."

	Regularly	Sometimes	Rarely
1. Children choose to play in the dramatic play center every day.	○	○	○
2. Children know and follow the rules for the dramatic play center.	○	○	○
3. The center is located away from quieter areas, such as the language and literacy center.	○	○	○
4. Materials are stored in labeled containers and shelves or on hooks within children's reach.	○	○	○
5. There are books about people engaged in a diverse range of occupations and activities.	○	○	○
6. There is enough space for children to move freely without bumping into objects or each other.	○	○	○
7. Children play individually, in pairs, and in small groups.	○	○	○
8. While using the dramatic play center, children express thoughts and feelings and build skills in all domains.	○	○	○
9. The dramatic play center includes props and dress-up items that			
• Encourage children to explore new roles, themes, scenarios, and challenges	○	○	○
• Incorporate other classroom activities	○	○	○
• Match the ages and skill levels of children in the class	○	○	○
• Respond to children's changing interests and experiences	○	○	○
10. Teachers extend children's play by			
• Engaging children in conversations	○	○	○
• Asking questions	○	○	○
• Responding to children's questions	○	○	○
• Offering ideas	○	○	○
• Commenting on children's explorations and creations	○	○	○
• Providing new props that offer different experiences and challenges	○	○	○

Credits

··

The following are selections published previously in *Teaching Young Children* and the issues in which they appeared:

Art

"The Value of Open-Ended Art," October 2013

"Art Learning Center," June 2010

"A Place for Weaving," February 2012

"Painting Without Brushes," August 2008

"Using Collage to Encourage Creativity, High-Level Thinking, and Conversation!" February 2012

"Books With Engaging Illustrations," February 2009

"Collecting, Painting, and Studying Leaves," December 2012

"Splatter Paint," August 2008

"How Children Discover Science While Exploring Art," October 2010

Music and Movement

"The Power of Creative Dance," October 2012

"Music and Movement Center," April 2011

"Making Musical Instruments," April 2013

"A Stage for a Playground: An Outdoor Music Center," October 2012

"Books That Feature Song Lyrics," October 2013

"Dance Stories," October 2012

"Going to a Live Performance," February 2011

"Listen, Sing, Play: Nature-Related, Low-Cost Music Activities," June 2011

"Eight Ways to Promote Music Play," February 2008

Dramatic Play

"Oral Storytelling: Building Community Through Dialogue, Engagement, and Problem Solving," October 2011

"Dramatic Play Center," February 2010

"A Place for Making Puppets," April 2012

"Nine Way to Make Puppets," February 2010

"Pretend Play Leads to Real-Life Learning," November 2007

"Books About Folktales," October 2012

"Creating and Using Prop Boxes," April 2009

"Engineering With *The Three Little Pigs*," February 2014

"Using Improvisational Play to Support Social Skills," December 2013

The following are adaptations of articles published previously in *Young Children* and the issues in which they appeared:

Music and Movement

"Young Children and Movement: The Power of Creative Dance," March 2010

"Theater, Live Music, and Dance: Conversations About Young Audiences," March 2010

"Music Play: Creating Centers for Musical Play and Exploration," July 2004

Dramatic Play

"Oral Storytelling: Building Community Through Dialogue, Engagement, and Problem Solving," December 2011

"Using Improvisational Play to Support Social Skills," December 2013

About the Authors

Lauren Baker is an assistant editor at NAEYC. She writes and edits for the magazine *Teaching Young Children*.

Jacqueline J. Batey is an assistant professor at the University of South Carolina in Bluffton, South Carolina. She teaches early childhood classes in art, music, and movement.

Doriet Berkowitz has co-taught in a preschool setting, and now teaches kindergarten and first grade in a multiage classroom at The Project School, a public charter school in Bloomington, Indiana.

Jolyn Blank is lives in Tampa, Florida. She is an associate professor of early childhood education at the University of South Florida.

Laura J. Colker, EdD, of Washington, DC, is president of L.J. Colker & Associates. In addition to being a contributing editor of *Teaching Young Children*, she has authored more than 100 publications and instructional guides, including co-authorship of *The Creative Curriculum for Preschool*.

Meghan Dombrink-Green received her master's degree from Johns Hopkins University and served as a Fulbright English Teaching Assistant to Cyprus. She is an associate editor at NAEYC, working primarily on *Teaching Young Children*.

Amy Laura Dombro develops resources to assist teachers, family support professionals, and community leaders in their work of creating positive change for children and families. Amy translates information so that it is engaging and easy to use and documents stories of successes, challenges, and lessons learned of individuals and programs so that readers can benefit from the experiences of others.

Connie Bergstein Dow, MFA, lives in Cincinnati, Ohio. She has published two books, *Dance, Turn, Hop, Learn! Enriching Movement Activities for Preschoolers* (Redleaf Press, 2006), and *One, Two, What Can I Do? Dance and Music for the Whole Day* (Redleaf Press, 2011). She teaches dance at the University of Cincinnati College Conservatory of Music Preparatory Department.

Susan Friedman is executive editor of digital content at NAEYC. She received her MEd from the Harvard Graduate School of Education. Formerly a preschool teacher, she has served as the editorial director for a number of educational websites.

Donna Furmanek, MEd, received her degree in early childhood leadership and advocacy from National Louis University, in Chicago. She is a National Board Certified Teacher, a Laban Certified Movement Analyst, and a presenter on the effects of movement in early childhood. Donna teaches kindergarten in the Chicago suburbs.

Lynn C. Hartle, PhD, lives in Media, Pennsylvania. She works at The Pennsylvania State University, Brandywine as professor of education.

Maureen Ingram lives in Silver Spring, Maryland. She is a preschool teacher at Inspired Teaching Demonstration School in Washington, DC.

Kristen M. Kemple lives in Gainesville, Florida. She is a professor of early childhood studies at the University of Florida.

Petra Kern, PhD, MT-DMtG, MT-BC, MTA, resides in Santa Barbara, California. She is the owner of Music Therapy Consulting and online professor at Marylhurst University and the University of Louisville.

Kara J. Ketter lives in Yorktown, Indiana. She works at the Indiana Association for the Education of Young Children as a quality advisor for the Indiana Accreditation Project.

Derry Koralek, NAEYC's chief publishing officer, oversees the development of the association's award-winning, research-based periodicals and books. She has worked at NAEYC for nearly 14 years and is the founding editor in chief of *Teaching Young Children*.

Leigh Tyler Marshall-Oliver resides in Charleston, Missouri. She is a service coordinator at County Disability Resources.

Christine Maynard, PhD, lives in Ames, Iowa. She teaches at Iowa State University as an assistant professor in the Department of Human Development and Family Studies.

Violet McGillen lives in Pittsburgh, Pennsylvania, and for the past eight years has been a preschool and kindergarten teacher at the Carnegie Mellon University Children's School. In her current role she substitutes for teacher absences, designs the whole school unit, and works on program enhancement projects.

Beth McLaughlin, LCAT, MT-BC, lives in Scotia, New York. She is the coordinator of music therapy services at Wildwood School in Schenectady, New York.

Carol Garboden Murray lives in New Paltz, New York. She is the director of the Abigail Lundquist Botstein Nursery School at Bard College and is a credentialed early learning trainer (NYSAEYC).

Barb O'Neill lives in Fresno, California. She works at CalState, Fresno as an assistant professor of early childhood education.

Michele J. Russo lives in the greater New York City area. She is a poetry coordinator at the Geraldine R. Dodge Foundation. Michele is a published author, an art enthusiast, the owner of a delirious shelter dog, and an all-around nature lover.

Triada Samaras, MA, MFA, is a transdisciplinary artist living, working, and exhibiting in New York City. She teaches art classes at Kean University and art education to preservice Pre-K–12 teachers at William Paterson University. In addition she is a William Paterson University Art Professor in Residence in the Paterson, New Jersey, public schools on a Dodge grant.

Sara Starbuck lives in Carterville, Illinois. She works at Southeast Missouri State University as an associate professor in the Department of Human Environmental Studies.

Janis Strasser lives in Ridgewood, New Jersey. A professor of early childhood education at William Paterson University, she frequently writes about the arts, diversity, and literacy in early childhood education. She has been a preschool, kindergarten, and music teacher, and a Head Start Education Coordinator and has been in the field for almost 40 years.

Ellie Wastin resides in St. Petersburg, Florida. She works for Pinellas County Schools as a preschool teacher.

TYC

TEACHING YOUNG CHILDREN/PRESCHOOL

Much of the content in this book is adapted from *Teaching Young Children* (*TYC*), NAEYC's award-winning magazine, which celebrates and supports everyone who works with preschoolers. Each issue presents practical information through text, photographs, infographics, and illustrations. Short, research-based articles share ideas to use right away.

TYC is available as a member benefit or through subscription. If you like this book, go to www.naeyc.org to join NAEYC or become a *TYC* subscriber.